101 ONE DISH DINNERS

------- HEARTY RECIPES -------
FOR THE DUTCH OVEN, SKILLET & CASSEROLE PAN

ANDREA CHESMAN

Storey Publishing

*The mission of Storey Publishing is to serve our customers by
publishing practical information that encourages
personal independence in harmony with the environment.*

Edited by Andrea Dodge and Carleen Madigan
Art direction by Jeff Stiefel
Book design and text production by Jackie Lay
Indexed by Andrea Chesman

Cover and interior photography by © Johnny Autry

Storey Publishing
210 MASS MoCA Way
North Adams, MA 01247
storey.com

Printed in China by Toppan Leefung Printing Ltd.
10 9 8 7 6 5 4 3 2 1

Library of Congress Cataloging-in-Publication Data

Names: Chesman, Andrea, author.
Title: 101 one-dish dinners : hearty recipes for the dutch oven, skillet, and
   casserole pan / Andrea Chesman.
Other titles: One hundred one one-dish dinners | One hundred and one one-dish
   dinners
Description: North Adams, Massachusetts : Storey Publishing, [2016] |
   Includes index.
Identifiers: LCCN 2016015559 (print) | LCCN 2016017687 (ebook) | ISBN
   9781612128412 (pbk. : alk. paper) | ISBN 9781612128429 (Ebook)
Subjects: LCSH: One-dish meals. | Casserole cooking. | LCGFT: Cookbooks.
Classification: LCC TX840.O53 C44 2016 (print) | LCC TX840.O53 (ebook) | DDC
   641.82--dc23
LC record available at https://lccn.loc.gov/2016015559

DEDICATED

To my family, always

CONTENTS

INTRODUCTION:
ONE DISH DOES IT ALL

We all know what "comfort food" means: honest, simple dishes made from scratch, using quality ingredients. It's cooking that is heavy in comfort, familiar, and dependable — no weird combinations, no challenging textures, no complicated procedures.

Your version of comfort food may be different from mine, though. When I was growing up, my mother started every single dish she cooked by sautéing an onion in vegetable oil. Her chicken soup with matzoh balls may have been as foreign to you as your mom's chicken and dumplings or tom yum soup would have been to me. Yet it is all instantly recognizable as comforting food, easily made at home.

America, it has been observed, is not really a melting pot. It's actually a huge potluck dinner, in which platters of roasted chicken beckon beside casseroles of pasta, mounds of tortillas, stew pots of gumbo, and skillets filled with pilafs of every imaginable color. And though all the delicious moussakas and curries and Chinese noodle dishes were once enjoyed only within specific immigrant enclaves, sometime within the past 50 years culinary borders between neighborhoods were breached, and home cooks started exploring the foods of other ethnic communities. Many of these dishes were one-pot meals: easy to make, easy to serve to families that scattered among meetings and work, school and Little League, music lessons and soccer games.

EARLY AMERICAN ONE-DISH DINNERS

Home cooks have always looked for easier ways to get a meal on the table. Early American cooking happened over the blistering heat of the wide-open kitchen fireplace, where an astonishing number of women met their untimely deaths when their long skirts and aprons caught fire. In those days, cooking was often done in a single pot that hung from a crane, slowly simmering, while women (who did most of the cooking then) went about doing a number of things: raising the children, tending the garden, cleaning the house, sewing the clothes, and attending to the livestock. There was much work to be done, and little time to be spent cooking.

FROM DUTCH OVENS TO SALAD BOWLS

From the Pilgrim hearth to the chuckwagon fire pit, much of what American cooks made was simmered or baked to perfection in a Dutch oven. The Dutch oven was developed in the early 18th century in England and Holland as a round-bottomed pot with flared sides that rested on three legs directly over live coals. It had a rimmed lid that was designed to hold more live coals and a handle for lifting or suspending the pot from a crane over the fire. When coals were placed on top of the lid, the heat surrounded the pot, and it was suitable for baking, as well as for cooking.

Dutch ovens were variously called "bake ovens," "bake kettles," and "camp ovens," as well as the more common "Dutch oven." Some historians believe that the name originated with German or Dutch peddlers who sold the cast-iron pots from their wagons. It is likely that the original cast-iron cookware was made in Holland and imported into England in the early 18th century, or it was manufactured in England and named after a Dutch casting technique that was patented in England in 1708.

Skillets, or frying pans, were also first made with legs, but like Dutch ovens, later became flat bottomed and lost the legs as the cookstove evolved. These were also made of cast iron and could go from stove to tabletop. The skillet was especially useful for frying everything from the morning's eggs to Sunday's fried chicken, as well as for baking cornbread and making roux for a gumbo.

Casseroles were once defined as a dish or pot in which food is baked and, often, served. The word, which may also refer to the food itself, is from the French and was first printed in English in 1708. Cooking in such dishes is rather ubiquitous. The idea of the casserole as a one-dish meal became popular in the United States around World War II, when all sorts of easy-to-prepare foods became popular. The 1943 edition of *The Joy of*

ONE-DISH TIP:
CARING FOR AND SEASONING CAST IRON

To season new cast iron, or to reseason an older pan, wash the pan in soapy water. Dry thoroughly. Brush the inside of the pan with a flavorless cooking oil or lard. Then add enough fat to measure ¼ inch deep in the pan. Heat the pan for 1 hour in a 300°F oven. Cool, pour out any excess fat, and wipe the pan clean with a paper towel.

Some people wash their cast-iron cookware in soap and water, dry the pan, and reseason it by brushing on more oil, heating briefly, then wiping the pan clean. However, if you do not use soap and water and simply wash the pan after use with a clean cloth, you can avoid this step. Burned-on foods can be released by scouring with salt before the pan is wiped clean. Cast iron will absorb food odors and flavors, so after cooking a strongly flavored dish, like curry, you may want to wash with soap and water and then reseason.

Cooking by Irma S. Rombauer called Tuna, Noodle, and Mushroom Soup Casserole an "excellent emergency dish." Cookbooks of the '50s, '60s, and '70s were filled with all manner of canned condensed soup and noodle mixes.

Today, home cooks in search of simplicity are just as likely to reach for salad bowls when feeding their families as soup pots or casseroles. Ever since pasta salads replaced tuna-macaroni salads on salad bars, we have made hearty salads for dinner. Interestingly, many of these salads are based on hot-dish classics. It turns out that rice and beans with the addition of a citrus-based vinaigrette makes a terrific one-dish salad supper. Curried chicken can be served cold with a chutney-based salad dressing. Chinese noodle dishes make excellent pasta salads dressed with soy-based vinaigrettes.

This collection of recipes looks both to the past and the present. It presents one-dish meals suited to today's busy cooks. Some soups and stews involve long simmering on the back of the stove or in the oven, largely unattended. These are good for weekend meals. The skillet suppers are all quickly made from scratch, most of them in well under an hour. Likewise, the salad suppers can be whipped together quickly. It's all good home cooking, with an eye on the clock.

COOKING ADVICE

Some 30 years ago, when my sister was married, she expected to give all her bridesmaids jewelry as thanks for services rendered, but I coveted a wedding gift she planned to return to the department store — a set of cast-iron skillets. She graciously presented me with the skillets, and I am happy to say both her marriage and my frying pans have endured.

Those skillets have accompanied me cross-country and back. They have been used to sauté shrimp in city apartments and fresh-caught trout over campfires. They were used to test almost every recipe in chapter 2 of this book, and I expect to pass them on to one of my kids when I'm no longer cooking for myself. Good cookware endures and inspires.

We don't have much extra time these days, so setting up a kitchen with the right cookware can make cooking go easily and smoothly. You don't need a lot of gadgets; you don't need a lot of different pots and pans. But do yourself a favor and buy the best that you can afford. If supper can be whipped together in minutes and cleaned up afterward so that you still have time for yourself or for playing with the kids, it will all be worth it.

GOOD CUTTING TOOLS

The larger the cutting board, the easier the chopping goes. You won't have food falling off the cutting board, and you may even have the room to leave the prepped food on the board instead of storing it in a bowl, which is just one more dish to clean later.

Sharp knives are a must. A good heavy chef's knife, a paring knife, a serrated knife for slicing tomatoes and bread, and a swivel-bladed vegetable peeler will cover just about every situation you will encounter. A carving knife is a nice acquisition, but you could get by without it.

QUALITY COOKWARE

For soups and stews, you will need a large, heavy-bottomed saucepan or Dutch oven. The most versatile ones can go from stovetop to oven. Cast-iron is good. Even better is porcelain-clad cast-iron; it has the good heat distribution of cast-iron but won't react to high-acid foods, such as tomato sauce.

For skillets, I recommend cast-iron. Once properly seasoned, it is reasonably nonstick and virtually impossible to destroy. Don't buy cast-iron skillets with wooden handles, though; the handles tend to break and then the pan is worthless.

For the oven meals, a 9- by-13-inch glass baking dish will cover almost every recipe in this book. The few that won't fit into a 9- by-13-inch dish require a large roasting pan, but you'll need that for Thanksgiving anyhow, right?

And that leaves salad suppers, for which you will need a large bowl. Simple.

STOCKING the PANTRY

Even when you cook from scratch, certain convenience foods can provide shortcuts that make the cooking go faster. The three convenience foods I rely on are canned tomatoes, beans, and broth. Feel free to substitute home-grown or home-cooked ingredients. Use 2 cups of chopped fresh tomatoes for 15 ounces of canned diced tomatoes with juice. Use 2 cups cooked dried beans for 15 ounces of canned. But if you use the canned goods, don't feel you are sacrificing flavor. Canned tomatoes are better than out-of-season supermarket tomatoes. And there are several commercial broths that are comparable to homemade. Taste several brands before settling on one. Canned beans should be drained and rinsed before they are used.

SOUPS AND STEWS

QUICK BLACK BEAN SOUP

SERVES 6

Black bean soups and stews are especially common throughout Latin America, the Caribbean, and the southern United States, particularly in Florida and in the Southwest. Using canned black beans makes it possible to whip up this soup at a moment's notice. The secret ingredient is chipotle chile, a smoked-dried jalapeño, which adds a whisper of smoke and just the right amount of heat. You could substitute 1 to 2 tablespoons minced canned chipotles en adobo. Just be sure to add the cup of water to thin the soup.

1 Combine the chipotle and boiling water in a blender. Let soak for 15 minutes.

2 Add the garlic and one-third of the beans to the blender. Process until puréed.

3 Heat the oil over medium-high heat in a large soup pot. Sauté the onion, bell pepper, fresh chile, if using, and 1 teaspoon cumin in the oil until the vegetables are limp, 3 to 4 minutes. Add the tomatoes, the remaining beans, and the puréed bean mixture. Season to taste with salt and pepper. Bring to a boil, reduce the heat, and simmer for 15 minutes to blend the flavors. Taste and adjust the seasoning, adding more salt, pepper, and cumin, if desired.

4 Serve hot, garnishing each bowl with a little cilantro.

1 chipotle chile

1 cup boiling water

2 garlic cloves

3 cans (19 ounces each) black beans, rinsed and drained

2 tablespoons extra-virgin olive oil

1 onion, diced

1 red bell pepper, diced

1 green chile, seeded and diced (optional)

1–1½ teaspoons ground cumin

1 can (28 ounces) diced tomatoes with juice

Salt and freshly ground black pepper

¼ cup chopped fresh cilantro

LENTIL SOUP

SERVES 6 TO 8

The most famous lentil soup of all time is the "mess of pottage" for which the biblical Esau sold his birthright. Lentils were probably one of the first food crops to be domesticated, dating back to the beginning of agriculture in the Fertile Crescent of the Middle East. We have been making lentil soup ever since.

1 Heat the oil over medium-high heat in a large soup pot. Sauté the onion, celery, carrots, and garlic in the oil until the onion is limp, about 3 minutes. Add the lentils, broth, and thyme. Bring to a boil, then skim off any foam that rises to the top. Reduce the heat, cover, and simmer until the lentils are mushy, 45 to 60 minutes, depending on the variety and age of the lentils.

2 Let cool slightly, then purée in a blender. Return to the pot and thin with additional water, if desired. Add the tomatoes and mixed vegetables.

3 Simmer for about 30 minutes, until the vegetables are tender. Season generously with salt and pepper. Stir in the parsley. Serve hot.

2 tablespoons extra-virgin olive or canola oil

1 onion, coarsely chopped

2 celery stalks, coarsely chopped

2 carrots, sliced

4 garlic cloves, halved

2 cups dried green or brown lentils, rinsed

6 cups vegetable or chicken broth (see pages 61–62) or water, plus more as needed

2 tablespoons chopped fresh thyme or 2 teaspoons dried thyme

1 can (28 ounces) diced tomatoes with juice

4 cups diced mixed fresh or frozen vegetables (such as green beans, carrots, corn, zucchini, and turnips)

Salt and freshly ground black pepper

¼ cup chopped fresh parsley

CURRIED RED LENTIL SOUP

SERVES 6 TO 8

The beautiful orange color of the red lentils fades to a mustard yellow-green as they cook, which is a pity. But as far as pottages go, the taste of this one is worthy of a birthright.

1 Combine the lentils, water, onions, carrots, ginger, cumin, garam masala, turmeric, 2 teaspoons salt, and 1 teaspoon pepper in a large soup pot. Bring to a boil, then skim off any foam that rises to the top. Reduce the heat, cover, and simmer until the lentils are very tender, 45 to 60 minutes. Let cool slightly.

2 Process the soup in a blender until smooth; you will have to do this in batches.

3 Return the soup to a soup pot. Stir in the hot sauce and coconut milk. Simmer for about 30 minutes. Taste and adjust the seasonings.

4 Just before serving, stir in the cilantro. Serve hot. Do not allow the soup to boil once the coconut milk has been added.

NOTE: To toast cumin seeds, place in a dry skillet over medium heat. Toast until fragrant, stirring occasionally, about 1 minute.

2½ cups dried red lentils, rinsed

8 cups water

2 onions, chopped

2 carrots, finely chopped

1 piece fresh ginger (1–2 inches long), peeled and sliced

1 tablespoon cumin seeds, toasted (see Note)

1½ teaspoons garam masala or curry powder

½ teaspoon ground turmeric

Salt and freshly ground black pepper

2 tablespoons hot pepper sauce, such as Frank's, or more to taste

1 can (13.5 ounces) coconut milk

¼ cup minced fresh cilantro

POTATO-LEEK SOUP

SERVES 4

Call it "potato-leek soup," and it is home-style comfort food. Call it "vichyssoise" and serve it cold, and it becomes an elegant soup first served at the Ritz-Carlton Hotel in 1917 and named after the city of Vichy, where Chef Louis Diat, the creator of the recipe, grew up. Substitute scallions for the leeks, and call it "shallot porridge," as French-speaking Louisianans do.

1 Combine the broth and potatoes in a medium saucepan, cover, and bring to a boil. Reduce the heat and simmer until the potatoes are tender, 15 to 20 minutes. Cool slightly.

2 Purée the potato mixture in a food processor or blender until smooth.

3 Heat the oil over medium-high heat in a large soup pot. Sauté the leeks in the oil until limp, about 4 minutes. Add the puréed potato mixture and half-and-half. Season to taste with salt and pepper. Simmer to blend the flavors, about 10 minutes.

4 Serve hot or cold.

5 cups chicken broth (see page 62)

2½ pounds russet potatoes, peeled and chopped

2 tablespoons extra-virgin olive oil or butter

4–6 leeks, trimmed and sliced

1 cup half-and-half

Salt and freshly ground black pepper

"In taking soup, it is necessary to avoid lifting too much into the spoon, or filling the mouth so full as to almost stop the breath."
— St. John the Baptist de la Salle
The Rules of Christian Manners and Civility (1695)

SPLIT PEA SOUP

SERVES 4 OR 5

Pease porridge hot, pease porridge cold, pease porridge in the pot, nine days old. This good, old-fashioned soup won't last that long. And when should you serve it? The second week of November has been National Split Pea Soup Week since 1969.

1 Combine the peas, water, and ham hock in a large soup pot. Bring to a boil, reduce the heat, and skim off any foam that rises to the top of the pot. Add the onions, celery, carrot, and bay leaf. Simmer for 1 hour.

2 Remove the soup from the heat to cool slightly. Remove the ham hock and bay leaf. Process the soup in a blender until smooth. Return to the pot.

3 Dice the meat from the ham hock, discarding the skin, bone, and fat. Add the meat to the soup. Season to taste with salt and pepper. Thin the soup with water, if desired. Heat through before serving. The soup improves in flavor and thickens on standing. Thin again with water, if desired.

2 cups dried split peas, rinsed
8 cups water, plus more to thin
1 smoked ham hock
2 onions, quartered
2 celery stalks, quartered
1 carrot, quartered
1 bay leaf
   Salt and freshly ground black pepper

VARIATION:
SPLIT PEA SOUP WITH SMOKED TURKEY

Lean smoked turkey contributes the flavor — but none of the fat — of the traditional ham hock. Add ½ pound smoked turkey, all in one piece, along with the onions, celery, and carrot. Remove before processing in the blender and finely dice. Return to the processed soup and season to taste with salt and pepper.

TUSCAN WHITE BEAN SOUP

SERVES 4 TO 6

With chicken stock on hand and canned beans, you'll need only about a half hour to make this delicious soup.

1 Heat the oil in a large soup pot over medium heat. Add the sausage and brown, breaking it up with a spoon as it cooks, about 5 minutes.

2 Add the broth, beans, carrots, garlic, and rosemary. Cover and bring to a boil. Simmer for 15 minutes, until the carrots are tender and the flavors have blended. Stir in the spinach. Simmer until wilted, about 2 minutes.

3 Season to taste with salt and pepper. Serve hot.

> "I live on good soup, not on fine words."
> — Jean-Baptiste Molière
> author of *Le Misanthrope* (1666)

2 tablespoons extra-virgin olive oil

½ pound hot Italian sausage, casings removed

4 cups chicken broth (see page 62)

2 cans (19 ounces each) cannellini beans, rinsed and drained

2 carrots, diced

4 garlic cloves, minced

1 teaspoon chopped fresh rosemary, or ½ teaspoon dried

4 cups chopped fresh spinach, tough stems removed (about 5 ounces)

Salt and freshly ground black pepper

PASTA E FAGIOLE

SERVES 6

The famous "pasta fazool" is an American colloquialism for this hearty soup of pasta and beans. Dean Martin immortalized it in his song, "That's Amore" ("When the stars make you drool just like pasta fazool, that's amore"). Made all over Italy, it's a soup with many variations. This version is quite simple, very quick to make, and very satisfying to enjoy.

1 Heat the oil in a large saucepan over medium-high heat. Sauté the onion and garlic in the oil until limp, about 3 minutes.

2 Add the broth, tomatoes, beans, rosemary, and oregano. Season generously with salt and pepper. Simmer for 10 minutes to blend the flavors.

3 Add the pasta and simmer until the pasta is tender, 10 to 15 minutes.

4 Serve immediately, passing the cheese at the table.

2 tablespoons extra-virgin olive oil

1 onion, diced

4 garlic cloves, minced

6 cups vegetable or chicken broth (see pages 61–62)

1 can (28 ounces) diced tomatoes with juice

1 can (28 ounces) cannellini beans, rinsed and drained

1 tablespoon chopped fresh rosemary, or 1½ teaspoons dried

1 tablespoon chopped fresh oregano, or 1 teaspoon dried

Salt and freshly ground black pepper

½ pound ditalini, tubettini, or other small soup pasta

Freshly grated Parmesan, to serve

MINESTRONE ALLA GENOVESE

SERVES 6

Minestrone translates as "big soup," which perfectly describes this hearty mixture of vegetables, beans, and pasta. The word is derived from *minestrare,* or "to administer," presumably because the soup was portioned out as the only dish served at a meal. There are as many versions of minestrone as there are cooks in Italy. What distinguishes minestrone from Genoa is the last-minute addition of pesto.

1 Heat the oil in a large soup pot over medium heat. Sauté the onion and garlic in the oil for 2 minutes. Add the broth, tomatoes, carrot, celery, fennel, thyme, and oregano. Bring to a boil, then reduce the heat and simmer for about 20 minutes.

2 Return the soup to a boil. Add the pasta and boil gently until the pasta is tender, about 10 minutes. Add the Swiss chard and beans. Simmer for 5 minutes longer, or until the greens are tender.

3 Add the pesto, if using, and season to taste with salt and pepper. Serve. The soup will thicken on standing. Thin with additional broth or water, if desired.

2 tablespoons extra-virgin olive oil

1 onion, diced

4 garlic cloves, minced

6 cups vegetable or chicken broth (see pages 61–62), plus more to thin (optional)

1 can (28 ounces) crushed tomatoes

1 carrot, diced

1 celery stalk, diced

1 fennel bulb, trimmed and diced

1 tablespoon chopped fresh thyme, or 1 teaspoon dried

2 teaspoons chopped fresh oregano leaves, or 1 teaspoon dried

1 cup small soup pasta (rings, ditalini, alphabets, bowties, etc.)

4 cups chopped Swiss chard, cabbage, or kale

1 can (15 ounces) cannellini beans, rinsed and drained

¼ cup pesto (optional)

Salt and freshly ground black pepper

"Beautiful soup, so rich and green
Waiting in a hot tureen!
Who for such dainties would not stoop?
Soup of the evening, beautiful soup!
Beautiful soup! Who cares for fish
Game, or any other dish?
Who would not give all else for two
Pennyworth of beautiful soup?"
— Lewis Carroll
Alice's Adventures in Wonderland (1865)

BARLEY MUSHROOM SOUP

SERVES 6

Barley is such an ancient grain that historians aren't really sure when and where it originated. Because it is a grain that is well suited to harsh climates, it has sustained cultures that arose in cold northern climates as well as desert dwellers. Today, most of the barley grown goes first to animal feed and second to the making of malt for beer. Only a small amount of barley is made into a grain for the kitchen, usually as pearled barley. Grinding the barley kernels with very abrasive disks creates pearl barley. Each time that the kernel is ground is called a "pearling." Before it is considered suitable for quick cooking, barley must go through three or four pearlings.

1. Place the dried porcini mushrooms in a small bowl. Pour the boiling water over the mushrooms and set aside to soak.

2. Combine the onions, celery, and garlic in a food processor. Pulse to finely chop. Set aside. Place 1 pound of the white mushrooms in the food processor and pulse to finely chop. Slice the remaining ½ pound.

3. Heat the oil in a large soup pot over medium heat. Sauté the chopped vegetables and chopped mushrooms in the oil until they are well browned and the liquid has mostly evaporated, about 15 minutes.

4. Add the broth, barley, and sliced white mushrooms to the soup pot. Add the soaked porcini mushrooms and their soaking liquid, avoiding any grit that has settled in the bottom of the bowl. Bring to a boil, then reduce the heat and simmer until the barley is tender, 40 to 60 minutes.

5. Stir in the sherry, dill, plenty of salt and pepper to taste, and parsley. Taste and adjust the seasonings. Serve hot.

1 cup dried sliced porcini mushrooms (1 ounce)

2 cups boiling water

2 onions, quartered

2 celery stalks, chopped

2 garlic cloves

1½ pounds white mushrooms

1 tablespoon extra-virgin olive or canola oil

8 cups vegetable or chicken broth (see pages 61–62)

⅔ cup uncooked pearl barley

¼ cup dry sherry

2 tablespoons chopped fresh dill, or 1 teaspoon dried

Salt and freshly ground black pepper

¼ cup chopped fresh parsley

"Soup puts the heart at ease, calms down the
violence of hunger, eliminates the tension of
the day, and awakens and refines the appetite."
— August Escoffier (1846–1935)

"But when that smoking chowder came in, the mystery was delightfully explained. Oh! sweet friends, hearken to me. It was made of small juicy clams, scarcely bigger than hazel nuts, mixed with pounded ship biscuits and salted pork cut up into little flakes! the whole enriched with butter, and plentifully seasoned with pepper and salt... we dispatched it with great expedition."
— Ishmael, speaking in Herman Melville's *Moby Dick* (1851)

NEW ENGLAND SEAFOOD CHOWDER

SERVES 4 TO 6

A New England-style seafood chowder is milk-based — never tomato-based — and generally includes potatoes and onions as well as seafood, which makes it a complete meal in a bowl. The key to a great chowder is to cook the seafood as briefly as possible, so that each spoonful contains meltingly tender seafood in a creamy rich broth.

1 Put the clams in a large pot with 2 cups water. Cover and bring to a boil over high heat. Cook, shaking the pot occasionally, until the clams begin to open, about 3 minutes. Remove the open clams and continue to cook for another minute or two, covered, removing more clams as soon as they open. Discard any clams that do not open.

2 Remove clams from their shells, holding them over a bowl to catch the juices. Chop the clams. Pour all broth and juice through a sieve lined with a coffee filter or paper towels into a glass measure; this should remove all the grit. Add enough water to measure 4 cups.

3 Cook the bacon in a large pot over medium heat until crisp, about 6 minutes. Remove the bacon with a slotted spoon and drain on paper towels.

4 Pour off and discard all but 2 tablespoons of the bacon fat. Add the onion and celery and sauté over medium heat in the remaining bacon fat until limp, about 3 minutes. Add the 4 cups clam liquid and potatoes. Bring to a boil, reduce the heat, and simmer until the potatoes are just tender, about 20 minutes.

5 Add the fish fillet and scallops to the pot. Simmer, covered, until the fish is just cooked, about 3 minutes. Add the cream and chopped clams. Season to taste with salt, if desired, and pepper. Heat just long enough to return the liquid to a simmer.

6 Serve in individual soup bowls, crumbling the bacon and sprinkling the parsley on top of each.

2 dozen hard-shell clams, scrubbed
Water
¼ pound bacon or salt pork, chopped
1 onion, diced
2 celery stalks, diced
1½ pounds potatoes, peeled and diced
½ pound white fish fillet, such as cod, cut into 1-inch chunks
½ pound bay scallops
1 cup light cream
Salt (optional) and freshly ground black pepper
¼ cup chopped fresh parsley

SEAFOOD GUMBO

SERVES 6 TO 8

Named for the Bantu word for okra, *gombo*, gumbo is a thick stewlike soup from Louisiana. A specialty born of the Creole cooking of New Orleans, gumbo often contains okra and a variety of meat or seafood. It usually includes a dark roux, a well-cooked paste of flour and oil, which thickens the stew and adds a silky texture, as well as a deep, rich background flavor. If okra is unavailable, substitute green beans or zucchini.

1. Heat the olive oil in a large pot. Sauté the onion, green pepper, celery, jalapeño, and garlic in the oil until the onion is limp, 3 to 4 minutes.

2. Add the broth, okra, sausage, tomatoes, parsley, bay leaves, thyme, cayenne, black and white peppers, and salt to taste. Bring to a boil, then simmer for about 30 minutes.

3. Meanwhile, combine the canola oil and flour in a medium frying pan, stirring until you have a smooth paste. Cook over medium-low heat, stirring, until the paste is a rich brown. This will take close to 30 minutes. Do not let the mixture burn; the darkened roux gives gumbo its characteristic flavor and color. If it burns, you must throw it out and start over again.

4. Carefully stir the roux into the gumbo, protecting your arms from hot spatters. Add the crabmeat, scallops, and shrimp. Taste and adjust the seasonings. Simmer for another 15 minutes, until the shrimp are pink and firm and the scallops are opaque. Taste and add more salt and pepper, if desired.

5. Remove the bay leaves. To serve, ladle the gumbo over the rice in large soup bowls. Pass the filé powder and hot sauce at the table.

- 1 tablespoon extra-virgin olive oil
- 1 onion, diced
- 1 green bell pepper, diced
- 2 celery stalks, thinly sliced
- 2 jalapeño chiles, seeded (optional) and diced
- 4 garlic cloves, minced
- 6 cups chicken broth (see page 62), or 4 cups chicken broth and 2 cups clam juice
- 1 pound okra, stems removed and pods sliced (about 4 cups)
- ½ pound andouille or other spicy smoked sausage, sliced
- 1½ cups diced tomatoes (fresh or canned)
- ¼ cup chopped fresh parsley
- 2 bay leaves
- 2 tablespoons fresh thyme leaves, or 1 tablespoon dried
- ½ teaspoon cayenne pepper
- ½ teaspoon black pepper
- ½ teaspoon white pepper
  Salt
- ¼ cup canola oil
- ¼ cup unbleached all-purpose flour
- 1 pound crabmeat
- 1 pound scallops
- 1 pound shrimp, peeled
- 4–6 cups cooked white rice, to serve
  Filé powder and Louisiana-style hot sauce, to serve

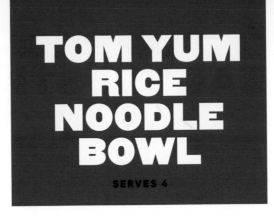

TOM YUM RICE NOODLE BOWL

SERVES 4

Thailand's delicate hot-and-sour soup served over rice noodles is possibly the world's finest bowl of steaming comfort. The soup has the odd quality of tasting more and more delicious as you eat. All of the exotic ingredients, including the rice noodles, are available wherever Asian foods are sold. Rice noodles are variable, however, so follow the directions on the package for cooking the noodles if they differ from the directions here.

1 Bring the broth to a boil over medium heat in a large saucepan. Add the lemongrass, lime leaves, ginger, and crushed red pepper. Reduce the heat, cover, and simmer for 15 minutes to allow the spices to infuse the broth. Remove the spices from the broth with a slotted spoon.

2 Meanwhile, bring a large pot of water to a boil for the rice noodles. (Be sure to follow the package instructions if they differ from the ones given here and in step 4.)

3 Add the shrimp, baby corn, mushrooms, snow peas, chile, lime juice, fish sauce, and sugar to the broth. Simmer for about 8 minutes, until the shrimp are pink and firm.

4 Meanwhile, add the rice noodles to the boiling water, remove from the heat, and let stand for about 8 minutes, until tender. Drain well.

5 Add the scallions and cilantro to the soup. Taste and adjust the seasonings, if needed. You should have an equal balance of spicy, sour, and salty. To serve, divide the noodles among the bowls. Pour the soup over the noodles and serve hot.

10 cups chicken broth (see page 62)

3 stalks fresh lemongrass, sliced on the diagonal into 2-inch pieces

4 kaffir lime leaves, or zest of 1 lime

1 piece fresh ginger or galangal (1-inch long), sliced

1 tablespoon crushed red pepper flakes

1 pound shrimp, peeled

1 can (14 ounces) baby corn, drained and cut into bite-size pieces

1 can (7 ounces) straw mushrooms, drained

1 cup snow peas or sliced bok choy

1 fresh green or red chile, seeded and thinly sliced

5 tablespoons fresh lime juice, or to taste

¼ cup Asian fish sauce, or to taste

2 tablespoons sugar

7–10 ounces rice sticks (¼-inch wide rice noodles)

4 scallions (white and tender green parts), sliced

¼ cup cilantro leaves

MEDITERRANEAN SEAFOOD STEW

SERVES 4 TO 6

A catch-of-the-day stew is a coastal favorite, no matter where the coast. This one has the characteristic flavors of the Mediterranean, though it bears a small similarity to gumbo. Serve with a crusty loaf of bread.

1 Heat the oil in a large saucepan or Dutch oven over medium-high heat. Sauté the leeks, bell pepper, fennel, shallots, and garlic in the oil until tender-crisp, about 5 minutes.

2 Add the tomatoes, fennel seeds, and broth. Bring to a boil, then reduce the heat and simmer for 10 minutes.

3 Add the clams to the broth, cover, and simmer for 5 minutes. Add the white fish and simmer for another 5 minutes. Then, add the shrimp, cover, and cook until the shrimp turn pink, about 5 minutes.

4 Stir in the pesto. Season to taste with salt and pepper. Discard any clams that have not opened. Serve at once.

> "Why does Sea World have a seafood restaurant? I'm halfway through my fish burger and I realize, Oh my God . . . I could be eating a slow learner."
> — Lyndon B. Johnson, former president of the U.S. (1908–1973)

¼ cup extra-virgin olive oil

2 leeks, sliced

1 red bell pepper, diced

1 fennel bulb, trimmed and diced

2 shallots, minced

4 garlic cloves, minced

3 tomatoes, seeded and chopped

1 teaspoon fennel seeds

4 cups chicken broth (see page 62) or fish broth

24 hard-shell clams or mussels

1 pound white fish, such as halibut, cod, snapper, or sea bass, cut into chunks

1½ pounds shrimp, peeled

¼ cup pesto, or ⅓ cup chopped fresh basil

Salt and freshly ground black pepper

CHINESE CHICKEN NOODLE BOWL

SERVES 4 TO 6

Comfort soup, Chinese-style. Throughout Asia, chicken soup is regarded as a healing food, prepared for the sick and for pregnant women, much like the "Jewish penicillin" of the West.

1 Combine the broth, ginger, garlic, sherry, and 2 teaspoons soy sauce in a large soup pot. Bring to a boil, reduce the heat, and simmer, uncovered, for 40 to 60 minutes, until the soup is fully flavored with the ginger and garlic.

2 While the soup simmers, bring a large pot of salted water to a boil. Cook the noodles in the water until just tender. Drain and toss with a few drops of sesame oil. Keep warm.

3 Remove the ginger and garlic from the soup with a slotted spoon. Season to taste with more soy sauce and salt, if desired. Add the chicken, greens, and baby corn. Simmer for about 15 minutes, until the greens are tender.

4 To serve, divide the noodles among the soup bowls. Pour in the soup, sprinkle with the scallions, and serve immediately.

> "Of Soup and Love,
> the first is best."
> — Thomas Fuller
> *Gnomologia* (1732)

8–10 cups chicken broth (see page 62)

1 piece fresh ginger (1-inch long), thinly sliced

3 garlic cloves, sliced

2 tablespoons dry sherry

2–3 teaspoons soy sauce

Salt

½ pound fresh Chinese egg noodles or dry vermicelli

Asian sesame oil

2 cups diced or shredded cooked chicken

4 cups chopped greens (bok choy, Chinese broccoli, Chinese mustard greens, kale)

1 can (14 ounces) baby corn, drained and cut into bite-size pieces

3 scallions (white and tender green parts), sliced

CHICKEN NOODLE SOUP

SERVES 6

Chicken noodle soup is one of the greatest of all comfort dishes. The vegetables add much in the way of nutrition and heartiness to the meal. Choose whatever combination of vegetables you like — carrots and celery are classics, corn adds a delicate sweetness, greens are bracingly tonic...

1 Bring the broth to a boil in a large soup pot. Add the chicken, vegetables, and egg noodles. Stir well and let simmer until the noodles and vegetables are tender, about 10 minutes.

2 Season to taste with salt and pepper. Serve hot.

8 cups chicken broth (see page 62)

2 cups cooked chopped or shredded chicken

4 cups mixed diced or shredded fresh or frozen vegetables (celery, carrots, parsnips, peas, green beans, corn, spinach, escarole, kale, in any combination)

6 ounces egg noodles (about 4 cups)

Salt and freshly ground black pepper

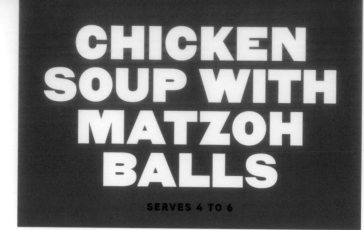

CHICKEN SOUP WITH MATZOH BALLS

SERVES 4 TO 6

Chicken soup with matzoh balls is an all-purpose cure — for a cold, the flu, or a broken heart. Matzoh balls are soup dumplings made from matzoh meal. Adding the chicken and greens is not classic, but it turns the soup into a complete meal.

1 Whisk together the oil, water, eggs, and salt in a medium bowl. Stir in the matzoh meal. Cover and refrigerate for at least 15 minutes.

2 Meanwhile, bring a large pot of salted water to a boil. Reduce the heat to medium-low to keep the water gently boiling.

3 Form the chilled matzoh-meal batter into 1-inch balls and carefully ease into the water. Cover the pot and boil gently for 30 to 40 minutes. The balls will fluff up and float to the top of the pot as they cook. The only way to tell if the matzoh balls are cooked is to remove one from the water and cut it in half. It should be firm and uniform in color — no wet, dark center. When the matzoh balls are done, remove from the pot with a slotted spoon.

4 Meanwhile, bring the broth to a boil in a soup pot with the parsley and the dill, if using. Add the greens and chicken, reduce the heat, and simmer, covered, until the greens are cooked through, 5 to 30 minutes, depending on the greens.

5 To serve, place 1 or 2 matzoh balls in each bowl and add the soup.

¼ cup canola oil

¼ cup water

2 eggs

1 teaspoon salt

1 cup matzoh meal

6–8 cups chicken broth (see page 62)

10 sprigs parsley

3 sprigs fresh dill (optional)

4 cups shredded greens (such as bok choy, chard, Chinese mustard greens, escarole, kale, or spinach)

2 cups diced cooked chicken

MOM'S
MATZOH BALLS

At some point in the evolution of matzoh balls, vegetable oil replaced chicken fat, or *schmaltz*, in the recipe. Olive and vegetable oils were scarce in Eastern Europe, so non-Jewish cooks used lard or butter as a cooking medium. For Jewish cooks, lard was out of the question because they were prohibited from eating pork products. Butter was acceptable only in dishes that contained no meat. That left chicken fat, which was cut from several chickens, then rendered by cooking it slowly with onion for flavor until it was reduced to a liquid. The fat was then strained and cooled before using.

Some say the lighter and fluffier the matzoh ball, the better. To make a lighter matzoh ball, use three eggs instead of two in the recipe opposite. To make a "cannonball," add more matzoh meal. But two people can follow the exact same recipe and come up with different results. Why? It is all in the handling. If you want to make light matzoh balls, don't compress the balls as you form them. Use two soupspoons to shape the mixture, and handle carefully. But note there is a fine line between light, fluffy matzoh balls and wimpy, easily crumbled ones. To make cannonballs, compress the mixture as though you were making meatballs.

CHICKEN BARLEY SOUP

SERVES 4 OR 5

Homemade chicken soup with whole-grain goodness. This is another recipe that assumes you have homemade chicken broth and cooked chicken on hand.

1 Heat the oil in a large soup pot over medium heat. Sauté the mushrooms and onion in the oil until the mushrooms have given up their juice, about 5 minutes. Add the broth, carrots, barley, and thyme. Bring to a boil, reduce the heat, and simmer, uncovered, for 45 minutes, until the barley is tender, stirring occasionally.

2 Add the chicken and parsley. Simmer for 5 minutes, until the chicken is heated through. Season to taste with salt and pepper and more thyme, if desired. Serve hot.

1 tablespoon extra-virgin olive oil or canola oil

2 cups mushrooms, finely chopped

1 onion, finely chopped

10 cups chicken broth (see page 62)

2 medium carrots, finely chopped

⅔ cup pearl barley

1 teaspoon chopped fresh thyme, or ½ teaspoon dried, or more to taste

2 cups cooked chopped or shredded chicken

¼ cup chopped fresh parsley

Salt and freshly ground black pepper

CHICKEN GUMBO

SERVES 6 TO 8

A cold gray day in Louisiana brings "gumbo weather," the perfect time for this highly spiced chicken stew. *Laissez les bons temps rouler!* (Let the good times roll!)

1 To make the chicken and broth, combine the chicken, onions, celery, and garlic in a large soup pot. Cover with the water. Bring just to a boil. Immediately reduce the heat and simmer gently for 2 hours with the lid partially on. Do not allow the soup to boil. Strain and discard the vegetables. Remove the meat from the bones and set aside. Discard the skin and bones. Chill the stock for several hours. Skim off the fat that rises to the top and hardens.

2 Heat the olive oil in a large soup pot. Sauté the onion, green pepper, celery, jalapeño, and garlic until the onion is limp, about 4 minutes.

3 Add 6 cups of the prepared broth, okra, sausage, tomatoes, parsley, bay leaves, thyme, black and white peppers, cayenne, and salt to taste. Bring to a boil, then simmer for about 30 minutes.

> Bridge City, Louisiana, claims to be the "Gumbo Capital of the World" on the basis of its annual gumbo festival, sponsored by the Holy Guardian Angels Roman Catholic Church on the first full weekend of October each year. At the festival, gumbo is cooked daily, and more than 2,000 gallons are served each year.

CHICKEN AND BROTH

3–4 pounds chicken parts

2 onions, chopped

3 celery stalks, chopped

3 garlic cloves, chopped

6–8 cups water

GUMBO

1 tablespoon extra-virgin olive oil

1 onion, diced

1 green bell pepper, diced

2 celery stalks, thinly sliced

2 jalapeño chiles, seeded (optional) and diced

4 garlic cloves, minced

1 pound okra, stems removed and pods sliced (about 4 cups)

1 pound andouille or other spicy, smoked sausage, sliced

1½ cups diced tomatoes (fresh or canned)

¼ cup chopped fresh parsley

2 bay leaves

2 tablespoons fresh thyme leaves

½ teaspoon black pepper

½ teaspoon white pepper

½ teaspoon cayenne pepper

Salt

4 Meanwhile, combine the flour and canola oil in a large frying pan, stirring until you have a smooth paste. Cook over medium heat, stirring, until the paste is a rich brown. This will take 20 to 30 minutes. Do not let the mixture burn; the darkened roux gives gumbo its characteristic flavor and color. If it burns, you must throw it out and start over again.

5 Carefully stir the roux into the gumbo, protecting your arms from hot spatters. Add the chicken. Taste and adjust the seasonings. Simmer for another 15 minutes. Remove the bay leaves.

6 To serve, ladle the gumbo over the cooked rice in large soup bowls. Pass the filé powder and hot sauce at the table.

¼ cup unbleached all-purpose flour

¼ cup canola oil

4–6 cups cooked white rice, to serve

Filé powder and Louisiana-style hot sauce, to serve

TOMATO CHICKEN SOUP

SERVES 4

The characteristic flavors of the sunny Mediterranean — tomato, olive oil, garlic, and rosemary — will cure whatever ails you. This recipe assumes that you have chicken broth (see page 62) and cooked chicken on hand, ready to be transformed into a delicious main-course soup.

1 Heat the oil in a large soup pot over medium-high heat. Sauté the mushrooms, onion, and green pepper in the oil for about 5 minutes, until the mushrooms begin to give up their juice. Add the garlic and sauté for another minute.

2 Add the tomatoes, broth, basil, rosemary, and thyme. Bring to a boil, then reduce the heat and simmer, uncovered, for 30 to 45 minutes, until the flavors have blended.

3 Add the chicken and heat through. Season to taste with salt and pepper. Serve hot.

2 tablespoons extra-virgin olive oil

2 cups white mushrooms, sliced

1 onion, thinly sliced

1 green bell pepper, diced

3 large garlic cloves, minced

1 can (28 ounces) plum tomatoes with juice, chopped

4–5 cups chicken broth (see page 62)

1 tablespoon chopped fresh basil, or 1 teaspoon dried

1 teaspoon chopped fresh or dried rosemary

1 teaspoon chopped fresh thyme, or ½ teaspoon dried

1½–2 cups cooked chicken, diced

Salt and freshly ground black pepper

CHICKEN & DUMPLINGS

SERVES 4 TO 6

There are many different ways to combine chicken and dumplings. Some cooks make a chicken soup — with or without vegetables — then plop down the dumplings on the soup. The dumplings absorb quite a bit of the broth, ending up extremely tender, but the dish is quite soupy. This version starts with a chicken fricassee — chicken in creamy sauce, which again could be made with or without vegetables (this version has plenty). It is topped with dumplings, which are then steamed on top of the stove, resulting in a dish that is not too dissimilar to chicken potpie.

1 Cover the chicken with water in a large pot. Add the onion, garlic, parsley, and peppercorns. Bring to a boil, reduce the heat, and simmer for 35 minutes, until the chicken is tender and no longer pink. Allow the chicken to cool in the cooking liquid.

2 Steam the carrots and green beans until just barely tender, 4 minutes. Drain.

3 When the chicken is cool enough to handle, remove it from the broth. Discard the skin and bones. Chop the meat into bite-size pieces.

4 Strain the broth and discard the solids. Skim off any fat that rises to the top. Reserve 4 cups broth for this recipe and refrigerate or freeze the remainder for other recipes.

5 To make the dumplings (ingredients on page 48), combine the milk and butter in a small saucepan and heat until simmering. Combine the flour, baking powder, and salt in a medium mixing bowl. Pour in the heated milk mixture and stir with a fork, until the mixture just comes together. Pinch off 18 walnut-size pieces and roll each into a 1½-inch ball.

CONTINUED ON NEXT PAGE

CHICKEN

4 pounds chicken parts, all white meat, all dark meat, or a mixture of white and dark meat

6–8 cups water

1 onion, quartered

2 garlic cloves, peeled and left whole

1 bunch flat-leaf parsley

1 teaspoon black peppercorns

2 carrots, diced

2 cups green beans, cut in 1-inch lengths

6 tablespoons extra-virgin olive oil

2 medium-sized leeks, trimmed and sliced

6 tablespoons unbleached all-purpose flour

2 tablespoons dry sherry

1 cup frozen peas

2 tablespoons chopped fresh dill, or 2 teaspoons dried thyme

Salt and freshly ground black pepper

6   Heat the oil in a large Dutch oven over medium heat. Sauté the leeks in the oil until tender, about 3 minutes. Sprinkle in the flour and stir until all the flour is absorbed into the oil. Whisk in the 4 cups reserved broth and the sherry, and stir until thickened and smooth. Stir in the chicken, carrots, green beans, peas, and dill. Season to taste with salt and pepper. Bring to a simmer.

7   Carefully lay the dumplings on the surface of the chicken mixture. Cover and simmer until the dumplings are cooked through, about 30 minutes. Serve hot.

DUMPLINGS

1 cup milk

3 tablespoons butter

2 cups unbleached all-purpose flour

1 tablespoon baking powder

¾ teaspoon salt

THE SHAPE
of DUMPLINGS

The origin of using small lumps of boiled or steamed dough to extend soups and stews is unknown to food historians, but it is a food of such simplicity that it probably evolved independently in peasant cuisines in various parts of Europe. The matzoh ball of chicken soup fame is one type of dumpling. Gnocchi, often made of potatoes, is another type.

In the U.S., dumplings may be made of wheat flour or cornmeal. If you grew up in the South, chances are your mom rolled out the dumpling dough thin and cut it into strips, or she rolled the dough thick and stamped out biscuit shapes. If your mom grew up in the Midwest or East, she probably shaped the dumplings into round balls. Is one way better than another? Does the dough have to accommodate these different ways of finishing? After much testing, the cooks at *Cook's Illustrated* concluded that either shape works just fine.

CHICKEN TORTELLINI SOUP

SERVES 4 TO 6

A quick soup for a cold night. Will knowing that the shape of the tortellini was inspired by Venus's navel make the soup more appealing?

1 Bring the broth to a boil in a large soup pot. Stir in the tortellini and cook until al dente. The timing will vary depending on the brand and whether the tortellini are fresh or frozen. The tortellini are done when they float to the surface.

2 Add the chicken and Swiss chard. Simmer until the chicken is heated through and the Swiss chard is wilted, about 5 minutes. Season to taste with salt and pepper, and serve.

10 cups chicken broth (see page 62)

¾ pound fresh or frozen cheese tortellini

2 cups cooked chicken

4 cups chopped Swiss chard or other greens

Salt and freshly ground black pepper

"Whoever tells a lie cannot be pure in heart — and only the pure in heart can make a good soup."
— Ludwig van Beethoven, letter to Mme. Streicher (1817)

CALDO VERDE

SERVES 4

Caldo verde ("green soup") is one of the national dishes of Portugal. It is a particular specialty of descendants of the Portuguese seamen who settled along the New England coast.

1 Combine the sausage and broth in a large saucepan. Bring to a boil, then reduce the heat and simmer while you prepare the potatoes.

2 Combine the potatoes with water to cover in a medium saucepan. Cover and bring to a boil. Boil until tender, about 8 minutes. Drain and briefly mash with a potato masher for an uneven, lumpy texture. Add to the chicken stock along with the kale.

3 Simmer for 10 to 15 minutes, until the kale is quite tender. Season to taste with salt and pepper.

4 Serve hot.

½ pound linguiça or chorizo sausage (or any garlicky smoked sausage), sliced

8 cups chicken broth, preferably homemade (page 62)

3–4 medium-sized potatoes (1 pound), peeled and diced

12 ounces kale, stems discarded and leaves chopped (8 cups lightly packed)

Salt and freshly ground black pepper

CHICKEN PROVENÇALE

SERVES 4 TO 6

Rich with the flavors of the Mediterranean, this chicken stew makes a fine one-dish meal. Be sure to serve it with a good loaf of crusty French bread to sop up all of the delicious sauce. A Côtes de Provence is a good choice for wine, and it can be used in the stew and for drinking with the meal.

1 Cut the chicken into small pieces (cut the breast into quarters; cut the thighs in half). Remove any fat, rinse, and pat dry. Place the flour in a shallow bowl. Season the flour with the salt and pepper and 1 tablespoon of the thyme. Dredge the chicken in the flour, shaking off any excess.

2 Heat the oil in a Dutch oven over medium-high heat. Add a single layer of the chicken and brown, turning as needed, about 10 minutes per batch. Adjust the temperature as needed to allow the chicken to brown but not scorch. (Make sure the chicken is well browned or the final dish will look anemic.) Remove the browned chicken to a bowl or plate and keep warm. Repeat until all of the chicken is browned.

3 In the oil remaining in the Dutch oven, sauté the onion, mushrooms, bell pepper, and fennel over medium-high heat, until the mushrooms have given up their juice, about 8 minutes.

4 Return the chicken to the Dutch oven. Add the tomatoes, wine, garlic, remaining thyme, and bay leaves, submerging the chicken in the liquid.

5 Cover and simmer until the chicken is tender and no longer pink, about 45 minutes, turning the chicken every 15 minutes or so.

6 Remove the chicken from the sauce with a slotted spoon and keep warm. Bring the sauce to a boil and boil until somewhat reduced, about 5 minutes.

7 Remove the bay leaves. Return the chicken to the pan. Taste and adjust the seasonings. Garnish with the parsley, and serve hot.

1 whole chicken, or 3½ pounds chicken parts

½ cup unbleached all-purpose flour
  Salt and freshly ground black pepper

2 tablespoons fresh thyme leaves, or 2 teaspoons dried

3 tablespoons extra-virgin olive oil

1 onion, halved and thinly sliced

4 ounces white mushrooms, sliced

1 green bell pepper, halved and sliced

2 fennel bulbs, trimmed and thinly sliced

2 cups seeded and diced tomatoes (canned or fresh)

½ cup red wine or chicken stock

2 garlic cloves, minced

2 bay leaves
  Chopped fresh parsley, to serve

ITALIAN WEDDING SOUP

SERVES 6

Greens and soup — particularly this combination of greens and meatballs in a clear broth — make a marriage made in heaven. Hence *minestra maritata* has been translated as "Italian wedding soup," though it was not necessarily served at wedding celebrations in Italy, where the recipe was developed. Greens can include escarole, chard, spinach, broccoli rabe, chicory, and cabbage, so feel free to use just one or a combination of these. This updated classic uses ground turkey in the meatballs, but the turkey can be replaced with the traditional ½ pound ground pork and ½ pound ground beef.

1 Bring the chicken broth to a simmer in a Dutch oven.

2 To make the meatballs, combine the ground turkey, eggs, bread crumbs, Parmesan, garlic, 1 teaspoon salt, and ½ teaspoon pepper in a food processor. Process until well mixed. Alternatively, mix by hand in a large bowl. Form the meat mixture into ½-inch meatballs (the size of marbles) and add to the simmering soup. Simmer until the meatballs are cooked through, about 30 minutes.

3 Increase the heat slightly, add the pasta, and boil gently until the pasta is cooked, about 10 minutes. Add the greens and continue to boil gently until the greens are tender, 3 to 10 minutes longer, depending on the type of greens. Taste and adjust the seasonings, remove from the heat, and serve.

12 cups chicken broth (see page 62)

1 pound ground turkey or ground pork

2 eggs

1 cup fresh bread crumbs

½ cup freshly grated Parmesan

2 garlic cloves, minced
   Salt and freshly ground black pepper

½ cup pastina or orzo (small pasta shapes)

1½ pounds greens, chopped

ONE-DISH TIP:

TIPS FOR MAKING MEATBALLS AND CLEANING GREENS

When making meatballs, you will find that the meat mixture will not stick to your hands if you keep your hands wet. Keep a bowl of water next to the meat mixture into which you can dip your hands from time to time.

When preparing greens, it is important to thoroughly wash them because the curly leaves can harbor dirt. Fill a basin with cold water, swish the greens around, then lift out of the water. Strip the leaves from tough stems and discard the stems.

"Talk of joy: there may be things better than beef stew and baked potatoes and home-made bread — there may be."
— David Gayson, American journalist, popular essayist (1870–1946)

BEEF STEW

SERVES 6

Does anything say "home cooking" better than a hearty bowl of beef stew?

1. Combine the flour, 1 tablespoon of the thyme, and the oregano in a medium bowl. Season generously with salt and pepper. Add the beef and toss to coat.

2. Heat 3 tablespoons of the oil in a large Dutch oven over medium heat. Lift the beef pieces out of the flour, shaking off the excess, and add a single layer of meat to the pot. Do not crowd the pot. Let the meat brown, turning as needed, about 5 minutes. Remove the meat as it browns and set aside. Continue cooking until all the meat is browned.

3. Add the remaining 1 tablespoon oil and the onion to the Dutch oven and sauté until the onion is soft, about 3 minutes. Add the broth, tomatoes, wine, garlic, and remaining thyme. Stir to scrape up any bits stuck to the bottom of the pot. Bring to a boil, then reduce the heat to a slow simmer. Return the meat to the pot. Partially cover the pot and let simmer until the meat is tender, about 2 hours.

4. Add the rutabagas, carrots, and potatoes to the pot and let simmer until the vegetables are tender, about 1 hour.

5. Add the peas and continue to simmer until the peas are heated through, about 5 minutes. Taste and adjust the seasonings. Serve hot.

⅔ cup unbleached all-purpose flour

2 tablespoons chopped fresh thyme leaves, or 1 tablespoon dried

1 tablespoon chopped fresh oregano leaves, or 1 teaspoon dried

Salt and freshly ground black pepper

2 pounds stew beef (chuck or round), cut into bite-size pieces

4 tablespoons extra-virgin olive oil

1 large onion, thinly sliced

1½ cups beef broth

2 cups diced canned tomatoes with juice

1 cup red wine

2 garlic cloves, minced

1 pound rutabagas or turnips, peeled and cut into 1-inch cubes

1 pound carrots or parsnips, cut into 1-inch cubes

1½ pounds potatoes, peeled and cut into 1-inch cubes

1 cup frozen peas or green beans (optional)

MOM'S BEST BOWL OF RED

SERVES 5 OR 6

Chili con carne is arguably one of the few truly American dishes. Jane and Michael Stern, in the introduction to their book *Chili Nation,* write, "We have come to believe that chili may just be this country's one truly shared national food. Although Tex-Mex in origin, it is a dish now found on every American table, across cultural and ethnic lines." This particular version is made with chunks of beef, as it is in Texas. But it also contains beans, which is decidedly *not* the Texan thing to do. It gets its heat from fresh hot chiles, ground chipotles, and plenty of ground chili powder, which, incidentally, was devised by a German immigrant in Texas in 1902 and did much to popularize the dish.

1 Combine the meat, chili powder, chipotle, cumin, and salt and pepper to taste. Toss to coat the meat with the spices.

2 Heat 1 tablespoon of the oil in a large skillet over medium heat. Sauté half the meat in the oil until browned, about 8 minutes. Transfer to a Dutch oven. Repeat with another 1 tablespoon oil and the remaining meat.

3 Heat the remaining 1 tablespoon oil in the skillet. Add the onions, bell peppers, and chiles, and sauté until softened, about 2 minutes.

4 Add the sautéed vegetables to the meat in the Dutch oven, along with the tomatoes and 2 cups of the water. Simmer over the lowest possible heat (do not boil), uncovered, until the meat is tender and the sauce is reduced and somewhat thickened, 2 to 3 hours. It is important not to rush the cooking; otherwise, the meat will be tough.

5 Stir in the beans and adjust the seasonings, adding more salt, pepper, cumin, or chipotle powder as needed. Mix the masa harina in a small bowl with the remaining ¼ cup water until dissolved. Stir into the chili and cook for about 5 minutes. Serve hot.

2½–3 pounds beef chuck, cut into ½-inch cubes

½ cup ground chili powder

1 teaspoon ground chipotle chile, or more to taste

1 teaspoon ground cumin, or more to taste

Salt and freshly ground black pepper

3 tablespoons extra-virgin olive oil

2 onions, finely chopped

2 red or green bell peppers, finely chopped

4–6 hot green chiles, finely chopped (seeding is optional)

1 can (28 ounces) diced tomatoes with juice

2¼ cups water

1 can (28 ounces) pink beans, pinto beans, or red kidney beans, rinsed and drained

1 tablespoon masa harina

"Wish I had time for just one more bowl of chili."
— Alleged dying words of mountain man Kit Carson (1809–1868)

VEGETABLE BROTH

14–16 CUPS

When you are cooking for vegetarians, you'll want to use a good vegetable broth rather than chicken broth for your soups. Most canned vegetable broths are dominated by one flavor — sometimes mushrooms, sometimes carrots, sometimes tomatoes. This broth is balanced in flavor and should serve as a good all-purpose foundation for soups, stews, and sauces.

1 Combine the carrots, leeks, onion, cabbage, fennel, garlic, parsley, thyme, and mushrooms in a large soup pot. Add the water. Cover, bring to a boil, then reduce the heat and simmer for 30 minutes.

2 Add the wine and peppercorns and continue to simmer, covered, for 10 minutes. Strain and discard all the solids.

3 Season to taste with salt, if desired. Use immediately or cool, then refrigerate. The broth will keep for about 5 days in the refrigerator or for up to 6 months in the freezer.

2 carrots, quartered
2 leeks, trimmed and quartered
1 large onion, quartered
¼ small head cabbage, trimmed and quartered
1 fennel bulb, trimmed and quartered
4 garlic cloves
1 bunch parsley
4 sprigs fresh thyme
1 cup dried porcini mushrooms
4 quarts water
1 cup dry white wine
1 tablespoon black peppercorns
Salt (optional)

ONE-DISH TIP:
FENNEL

To prepare fennel for cooking, slice off the root end. Then slice off the stalks, leaving the bulb, which is layered. Remove all tough or blemished layers from the bulb, usually the outermost layer. Cut the bulb in half and remove the core. Then slice or cut into wedges, as required by the recipe. Save a few fronds for a garnish.

CHICKEN BROTH

8–12 CUPS

Save chicken parts, such as wings, backs, and necks, for making stock. If you are buying chicken specifically to make broth, buy dark meat. It is less expensive than white meat and more flavorful. The additional fat in the dark meat will be skimmed off and discarded. As a bonus, the recipe yields 6 to 8 cups cooked chicken that can be used in soups, salads, or any dishes calling for cooked chicken.

1 Combine the chicken, onion, celery, garlic, and parsley in a large soup pot. Add the water. Cover and bring just to a boil. Immediately reduce the heat and simmer gently for 2 hours with the lid partially on. Do not allow the soup to boil.

2 Strain and discard the vegetables. Remove the meat from the bones and save the meat for another use, such as chicken salad.

3 Season the broth to taste with salt.

4 Refrigerate the broth for several hours. Skim off the fat that rises to the top and hardens.

5 Use immediately or store in the refrigerator for up to 3 days, or in the freezer for up to 6 months.

3–4 pounds chicken parts
1 large onion, quartered
4 celery stalks, quartered
4 garlic cloves
1 bunch parsley
4 quarts water
Salt

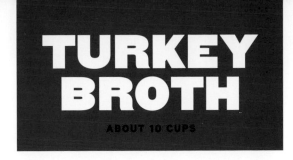

TURKEY BROTH

ABOUT 10 CUPS

Making good use of leftovers is a skill worth acquiring. Here's how to make soup stock from a leftover turkey carcass. Turkey broth can be used in place of chicken broth in any recipe.

1 Break the carcass into four or five pieces. Cover with the water in a large soup pot. Add the carrot, onions, celery, garlic, parsley, and bay leaf. Bring to a boil. Reduce the heat and simmer for 1½ hours.

2 Remove the turkey pieces and strain the liquid through a sieve, pressing on the solids to extract as much flavor as possible. Season to taste with salt.

3 Remove any meat from the bones and finely chop. Add to soups or make into turkey salad.

4 Refrigerate for up to 3 days or freeze for up to 5 months. Remove the layer of fat that hardens on the surface of the broth before heating and using.

1 carcass from a roasted turkey
16 cups water (roughly)
1 carrot, quartered
2 onions, quartered
4 celery stalks, quartered
4 garlic cloves
1 bunch parsley
1 bay leaf
Salt (optional)

SKILLET
SUPPERS

LOUISIANA RED BEANS & RICE

SERVES 4 TO 6

In Louisiana, red beans and rice was a traditional Monday night supper for two reasons. Monday was wash day, and cooks needed a supper that didn't require a lot of preparation. And, the beans could be flavored with a ham bone left over from Sunday's ham. Here's a quick vegetarian version of Louisiana red beans and rice. If you prefer, cut up any cured smoked sausage, such as andouille, and add it to the beans.

1 Heat the oil over medium-high heat in a large skillet. Sauté the onions, celery, bell peppers, chiles, and garlic in the oil until the onions are soft, about 5 minutes.

2 Add the broth, beans, thyme, bay leaves, hot sauce, and salt and black and white pepper to taste. Simmer until the beans are hot and the flavors have blended, about 15 minutes. Discard the bay leaves. Taste and adjust the seasoning.

3 Serve over the rice, passing more hot sauce at the table.

2 tablespoons extra-virgin olive oil

2 onions, diced

4 celery stalks, diced

2 green bell peppers, diced

2 green chiles, seeded (optional) and diced

4 garlic cloves, minced

2 cups vegetable or chicken broth (see pages 61–62), or water

6 cups cooked red kidney beans (or two 29-ounce cans, drained and rinsed)

2 tablespoons chopped fresh thyme leaves, or 2 teaspoons dried

2 bay leaves

2 tablespoons Louisiana-style hot sauce, such as Frank's, or more to taste

Salt and freshly ground black pepper

White pepper

4 cups hot, cooked long-grain white rice

ONE-DISH TIP:
CHOOSING SKILLETS

For the recipes in this book, you will need a large cast-iron or nonstick skillet or frying pan — one 12 inches in diameter or larger will work best. A heavy pan will conduct heat evenly so there are no hot spots where food may scorch. Copper and cast iron are good heat conductors. Stainless steel is often sandwiched with copper for better heat conducting. Look for a skillet with ovenproof handles so you can put it in the oven. A tight-fitting lid is essential.

TEX-MEX BLACK BEAN CORNBREAD SUPPER

SERVES 4 OR 5

What do cowboys eat for supper? Beans and biscuits. Here's a variation that pleases all the cowboys and girls.

1 Preheat the oven to 425°F.

2 To prepare the beans, heat the oil in a large oven-proof skillet over medium-high heat. Add the onion, bell peppers, chiles, and cumin. Sauté until the onion is soft, 3 to 5 minutes. Stir in the tomatoes, beans, and cilantro, if using. Cook for 1 minute more. Remove from the heat and season to taste with salt and pepper.

3 To prepare the cornbread topping, mix together the cornmeal, flour, sugar, baking powder, and salt in a medium bowl. In a small bowl, beat together the egg, milk, and oil. Pour into the cornmeal mixture and stir just until moistened. The batter will be lumpy. Spread the batter as evenly as possible over the beans in the skillet.

4 Bake for 20 to 25 minutes, until the top is golden and firm. Let stand for about 5 minutes before serving.

BEANS

2 tablespoons canola or extra-virgin olive oil

1 onion, finely diced

½ green bell pepper, finely diced

½ red bell pepper, finely diced

1–3 fresh hot red or green chiles, finely diced

2 teaspoons ground cumin

1 can (15 ounces) diced tomatoes with juice

1 can (15 ounces) black beans, rinsed and drained

2 tablespoons chopped fresh cilantro (optional)

Salt and freshly ground black pepper

CORNBREAD TOPPING

1 cup yellow cornmeal

¾ cup unbleached all-purpose flour

2 tablespoons sugar

2 teaspoons baking powder

1 teaspoon salt

1 egg

1 cup milk

2 tablespoons canola oil

BARBECUED BEAN CORNBREAD SUPPER

SERVES 4

Southern-style barbecued beans are paired with a corn-studded cornbread. The beans and cornbread are sweetly flavored, so a crisp slaw in a vinegar dressing makes the perfect accompaniment. The cornbread batter should be spread as evenly as possible, bringing it all the way to the rim of the pan to seal in the beans.

1 Preheat the oven to 425°F.

2 To prepare the beans, heat the oil in a large oven-proof skillet over medium-high heat. Sauté the onion, bell pepper, chiles, and chili powder in the oil until the onion is soft, 3 to 5 minutes. Stir in the beans, barbecue sauce, and water. Cook for 1 minute more. Remove from the heat and season to taste with salt and pepper.

3 To prepare the cornbread topping, mix together the cornmeal, flour, sugar, baking powder, and salt in a medium bowl. In a small bowl, beat together the egg, milk, and oil. Pour into the cornmeal mixture along with the corn and stir just until moistened. The batter will be lumpy. Spread the batter as evenly as possible over the beans in the skillet.

4 Bake for about 20 minutes, until the top is golden and firm. Let stand for about 5 minutes before serving.

BEANS

- 2 tablespoons canola or extra-virgin olive oil
- 1 onion, finely diced
- 1 green bell pepper, finely diced
- 1–3 fresh hot red or green chiles, finely diced (optional)
- 1 teaspoon ground chili powder
- 1 can (15 ounces) kidney beans, rinsed and drained
- 2/3 cup tomato-based barbecue sauce
- 1/3 cup water
  Salt and freshly ground black pepper

CORNBREAD TOPPING

- 1 cup yellow cornmeal
- 3/4 cup unbleached all-purpose flour
- 1 tablespoon sugar
- 2 teaspoons baking powder
- 1 teaspoon salt
- 1 egg
- 1 cup milk
- 2 tablespoons canola oil
- 1½ cups fresh or frozen corn kernels

RED RICE & BLACK BEANS

SERVES 4

What is known as "red rice" in the South is called "Spanish rice" in the rest of the United States. Like many Southern specialties, this dish probably originated in Africa. Red rice bears a striking resemblance to "jollof rice," which has its origins in West Africa. Although there are many variations of jollof rice, the most common basic ingredients are rice, tomatoes and tomato paste, onion, salt, and red pepper. Beyond that, nearly any kind of meat, fish, vegetable, or spice is used. This is a vegetarian version, using black beans to provide a color and flavor contrast. Chicken or shrimp can be used instead.

1 Wash the rice in at least two changes of water. Drain well.

2 Heat the oil in a large skillet over medium-high heat. Sauté the rice, onion, bell pepper, chiles, chili powder, and cumin in the oil, stirring constantly, until the rice appears opaque and toasted and the onion is softened, 5 to 8 minutes.

3 Drain the tomatoes, pouring the juice into a large glass measure. Add enough boiling water to the juice to make 4 cups. Add this liquid along with the tomatoes and salt and pepper to taste to the skillet. Stir well.

4 Cover, bring to a boil, reduce the heat, and boil gently until the liquid is fully absorbed, about 15 minutes.

5 Fluff the rice with a fork. Stir in the black beans and cilantro. Taste and adjust the seasonings. Serve at once.

2 cups long-grain white rice

2 tablespoons extra-virgin olive oil or canola oil

½ onion, finely chopped

½ green bell pepper, finely chopped

1–2 green chiles, seeded (optional) and finely chopped

1 tablespoon chili powder

1 teaspoon ground cumin

1 can (15 ounces) diced tomatoes with juice

Boiling water

Salt and freshly ground black pepper

1 can (15 ounces) black beans, rinsed and drained

¼–½ cup chopped fresh cilantro

RISOTTO PRIMAVERA

SERVES 4

Risottos are made by slowly adding broth to short-grain rice while stirring. The result is a creamy textured dish, very soothing and comforting. Any vegetables can be added to risotto, and this combination of spring vegetables is especially pleasing. Arborio rice, imported from Italy, is perfect for making a creamy risotto, but any short-grain rice will do.

1 Heat the broth and wine to simmering in a medium saucepan.

2 Bring a medium pot of salted water to a boil. Add the asparagus and peas and blanch for 1 minute. Drain and rinse under cold water to stop the cooking.

3 Heat the oil in a large skillet over medium-high heat. Add the rice, bell pepper, and garlic and toss to coat with the oil. Sauté for 3 to 5 minutes, until the rice appears opaque and the bell pepper is softened.

4 Add 1 cup of the simmering broth mixture to the rice and reduce the heat under the skillet to medium. Stir until the liquid is mostly absorbed. Continue adding broth, 1 cup at a time, cooking and stirring as the liquid is absorbed. It will take 18 to 25 minutes for all the liquid to be absorbed; the rice should have a firm but creamy consistency.

5 Stir in the asparagus, peas, and Parmesan. Season to taste with salt and pepper. Stir in the basil. Cover and let stand for about 3 minutes to allow the vege- tables to heat through. Serve at once.

5½ cups vegetable or chicken broth (see pages 61–62)

½ cup white wine

1 pound asparagus, trimmed and cut into 1-inch pieces

1 cup fresh or frozen peas

1 tablespoon extra-virgin olive oil

1½ cups Arborio or other short-grain white rice

½ red bell pepper, diced

2–3 garlic cloves, minced

¼ cup freshly grated Parmesan
Salt and freshly ground black pepper

6 basil leaves, cut into ribbons, or 1–2 teaspoons finely minced lemon zest

SAFFRON RISOTTO WITH SHRIMP & FENNEL

SERVES 4

The anise-flavored fennel and shrimp provide wonderful foils for the saffron-infused rice in this classic risotto. Fennel — also called Florence fennel or *finocchio* — is an odd-looking vegetable. It has a white, bulbous base, from which green stalks arise. The stalks sport feathery, dark green fronds. The bulb is what is eaten, the stalks are trimmed away (a few may be added to stock), and the feather fronds are used as an herb or garnish for dishes in which the bulb is featured.

1 Combine the broth, clam juice, and saffron in a medium saucepan and heat to barely simmering over low heat.

2 Heat the oil in a large skillet over medium heat. Sauté the fennel and shallots in the oil until the fennel softens, about 3 minutes. Add the rice and garlic and continue to sauté for 3 to 5 minutes, until the rice appears opaque.

3 Add 1 cup of the broth mixture to the rice. Simmer, stirring frequently, until most of the liquid is absorbed. Continue adding broth, 1 cup at a time, cooking and stirring as the liquid is absorbed. It will take 18 to 25 minutes for all the liquid to be absorbed; the rice should have a firm but creamy consistency.

4 Stir in the shrimp, tomatoes, and 1 tablespoon of the fennel leaves. Cover and cook over low heat until the shrimp are pink and firm, about 5 minutes.

5 Season to taste with salt and pepper. Serve immediately, garnishing with the remaining fennel leaves.

3 cups chicken broth (see page 62)

2½ cups bottled clam juice or chicken broth

¼ teaspoon crushed saffron threads

2 tablespoons extra-virgin olive oil

1 fennel bulb, diced

2 shallots, minced

1½ cups Arborio or other short-grained white rice

2 garlic cloves, minced

1 pound shrimp, peeled

2 tomatoes, seeded and chopped, or 1 cup canned diced tomatoes, well drained

2 tablespoons chopped fennel leaves

Salt and freshly ground black pepper

SKILLET CHOUCROUTE GARNI

SERVES 4 OR 5

Choucroute is the French word for sauerkraut. In a traditional choucroute garni, the sauerkraut is flavored with goose fat, onions, juniper berries, and white wine and served with potatoes and a variety of meats, including goose, pork, and ham. This skillet version omits both the goose fat and the hard-to-find juniper berries. Low-fat turkey sausage and smoked turkey breast replace the traditional fatty meats. Serve with a loaf of hearty rye or pumpernickel bread.

1 Cover the potatoes with salted water in a medium saucepan and bring to a boil. Let boil for 1 minute, then drain.

2 Heat the oil in a large skillet over medium-high heat. Sauté the sausage and onion in the oil until the sausage is browned, about 8 minutes.

3 Add the broth, sauerkraut, ham, carrots, bay leaves, peppercorns, and potatoes. The skillet will be quite full; stir carefully. Bring to a boil, reduce the heat, cover, and simmer for about 20 minutes, until the carrots and potatoes are tender.

4 Remove the bay leaves and let stand for about 5 minutes before serving.

1½ pounds red potatoes, sliced 1½ inches thick

1 tablespoon extra-virgin olive oil

½ pound smoked turkey or pork sausage, such as kielbasa, sliced

1 onion, thinly sliced

2 cups chicken broth (see page 62)

1½ pounds sauerkraut, drained and rinsed

½ pound smoked ham or turkey breast, cut into ½-inch cubes

4 carrots, sliced ½ inch thick

3 bay leaves

½ teaspoon peppercorns

SEAFOOD PAELLA

SERVES 4

There are probably as many paella recipes in Spain as there are cooks, but all are luxuriously scented with saffron. This variation relies on seafood: monkfish, shrimp, scallops, and clams. Consider the seafood used in this recipe as recommendations only; select whatever is fresh at the market, but do include some shellfish for a dramatic presentation.

1 Combine the broth and saffron and set aside.

2 Heat the oil over medium-high heat in a large oven-proof skillet. Sauté the rice, shallots, bell pepper, and garlic in the oil until the rice appears opaque and the bell pepper is softened, about 5 minutes.

3 Add the broth mixture, reduce the heat to maintain a gentle boil, cover, and cook until the liquid is absorbed and the rice is tender, about 15 minutes. Meanwhile, preheat the oven to 350°F.

4 When the rice is cooked, fluff with a fork. Stir in the peas. Season to taste with salt and pepper. Place the monkfish, shrimp, scallops, and clams on top of the rice. Cover and bake for 15 to 20 minutes, until the shrimp are firm and the clam shells open (discard any that are unopened).

5 Serve immediately, placing a lemon wedge on each plate.

4	cups chicken broth (see page 62)
½	teaspoon crushed saffron threads
2	tablespoons extra-virgin olive oil
2	cups medium-grain white rice
3	shallots, minced
1	red bell pepper, diced
3	garlic cloves, minced
1	cup fresh or frozen peas
	Salt and freshly ground black pepper
¼–⅓	pound monkfish, flounder, sole, or other white fish (1 fillet), cut into bite-size pieces
½	pound shrimp, peeled
¼	cup bay scallops
18	clams or mussels, well-scrubbed
1	lemon, cut into wedges

DOMINICAN SHRIMP & YELLOW RICE

SERVES 4

Rice, shrimp, and tomatoes are a classic combination in many different cuisines. In this pilaf from the Dominican Republic, the flavor accents come from cilantro and annatto, a seasoning that gives the rice a yellow color and a distinctive, almost floral flavor. You can find the brick-red seeds wherever Hispanic foods are sold; they are sometimes called *achiote*. Saffron can be substituted for the annatto (add ¼ teaspoon to the chicken broth) but the flavor will be different — Old World, not New World.

1 Wash the rice in at least two changes of water. Drain and set aside.

2 Combine the oil and annatto seeds in a large skillet. Cook over medium heat for 3 to 5 minutes to release the aroma (the fresher the seeds, the briefer the cooking time needed). With a slotted spoon, remove the seeds and discard.

3 Add the shrimp to the oil. Sauté until just pink and firm, about 3 minutes. With a slotted spoon, transfer the shrimp to a plate and keep warm. Add the onion, garlic, and rice to the oil and sauté until the onion is translucent and the rice appears dry and toasted, 3 to 5 minutes. Stir in the broth and bay leaves. Cover, bring to a boil, reduce the heat to maintain a gentle boil, and cook until all the liquid is absorbed, about 15 minutes.

4 Remove the bay leaves. Fluff the rice with a fork. Stir in the tomatoes, cilantro, and shrimp. Season to taste with salt and pepper.

5 Serve hot, passing the hot sauce at the table.

2 cups long-grain white rice

2 tablespoons extra-virgin olive oil

1 tablespoon annatto seeds

1 pound large shrimp, peeled

1 onion, finely chopped

3 cloves garlic, minced

4 cups chicken broth (see page 62)

2 bay leaves

2 medium-sized tomatoes, seeded and chopped

2 tablespoons chopped fresh cilantro

Salt and freshly ground black pepper

Hot pepper sauce, to serve

SHRIMP PILAU

SERVES 4

Sweet and hot peppers, along with cilantro and ham, make this Caribbean-inspired combination of rice and shrimp a festival of flavors. If neither asparagus nor green beans are in season, substitute 1½ cups frozen peas and do not blanch. Add to the rice with the shrimp.

1 Wash the rice in at least two changes of water. Drain and set aside.

2 Heat the oil in a large skillet over medium-high heat. Sauté the onion, garlic, bell pepper, chiles, and ham in the oil until the vegetables are limp, 3 to 5 minutes. Add the rice and sauté for another 3 to 5 minutes, until the rice appears opaque.

3 Stir in the broth and water. Season to taste with salt and pepper. Cover, reduce the heat to maintain a gentle boil, and cook for about 15 minutes, until the liquid is absorbed.

4 While the rice cooks, blanch the asparagus in boiling water to cover for 1 minute. Drain and set aside.

5 When the rice is cooked, fluff with a fork. Stir in the shrimp. Cover and cook over low heat for 3 to 5 minutes, until the shrimp is pink and firm. Stir in the asparagus and cilantro. Taste and adjust the seasonings. Serve at once.

2 cups long-grain white rice

2 tablespoons extra-virgin olive oil

1 onion, minced

2 cloves garlic, minced

1 green bell pepper, minced

1–2 fresh green or red chiles, seeded (optional) and minced

½ cup diced ham or Canadian bacon

2 cups chicken broth (see page 62)

2 cups water

Salt and freshly ground black pepper

1 pound asparagus or green beans, cut into 1-inch pieces

1 pound shrimp, peeled

¼ cup chopped fresh cilantro

PAD THAI

SERVES 4

Pad Thai — noodles with shrimp and peanuts — is one of Thailand's national dishes, sure to be found on the menu of any Thai restaurant you visit in this country. But there's no reason not to enjoy it at home. A combination of lime juice and molasses stands in for the hard-to-find tamarind to give this dish its characteristic sweet flavor.

1 Soften the rice sticks by soaking in cold water to cover for 30 minutes. Drain and set aside.

2 Meanwhile, make the sauce by combining the water, fish sauce, lime juice, molasses, sugar, and red pepper flakes. Set aside.

3 Heat the oil in a large skillet over medium-high heat. Sauté the shrimp, garlic, and ginger in the oil until the shrimp are pink and firm, about 3 minutes. Remove the shrimp from the skillet with a slotted spoon and keep warm.

4 Pour the eggs into the skillet. When the bottom of the eggs has set, about 15 to 30 seconds, add the drained noodles and sauce and stir-fry or toss with two spoons until the eggs are cooked through and the noodles have absorbed most of the liquid, about 5 minutes. Carefully mix in the shrimp, peanuts, 1 cup of the bean sprouts, and the scallions.

5 Garnish with the remaining bean sprouts and the cilantro and lime wedges. Serve hot.

¾ pound rice sticks (¼-inch flat rice noodles)

1¾ cups water

½ cup Asian fish sauce

¼ cup fresh lime juice

¼ cup molasses

5 tablespoons sugar

½ teaspoon crushed red pepper flakes

1 tablespoon peanut or canola oil

¾ pound shrimp, peeled

2 garlic cloves, minced

1 piece fresh ginger (1 inch long), peeled and minced

2 eggs, lightly beaten

¼ cup dry-roasted peanuts

2 cups bean sprouts

2 scallions, white and tender green parts, chopped

2 tablespoons chopped fresh cilantro

1 lime, cut into wedges

LOUISIANA-STYLE SHRIMP & RICE

SERVES 4

Don't be put off by the long ingredient list; this recipe is easy to prepare. The rich Louisiana-style flavor depends on the interaction of ingredients: sweet and hot peppers, onion, celery, garlic, black and white pepper, and thyme. You can make shrimp stock by simmering shrimp shells in water to cover for about 20 minutes, then strain — but bottled clam juice will do. Likewise, chicken broth adds richness, but water can be substituted.

1 Wash the rice in at least two changes of water. Drain and set aside.

2 Heat the oil over medium-high heat in a large skillet. Sauté the celery, green pepper, red pepper, chiles, and onion in the oil for about 5 minutes, until the vegetables are softened. Add the garlic and rice. Sauté for another 3 to 5 minutes, until the rice appears opaque. Add the shrimp broth, chicken broth, thyme, white pepper, black pepper, bay leaves, and hot pepper sauce. Cover and bring to a boil. Reduce the heat to maintain a gentle boil and cook for about 15 minutes, until the liquid is absorbed.

3 Remove the bay leaves. Fluff the rice with a fork. Stir in the shrimp, scallions, and parsley. Cover and cook for 5 to 7 minutes, or until the shrimp are pink and firm.

4 Season to taste with salt; taste again and adjust the seasonings, adding more hot pepper sauce, if desired. Serve hot.

- 2 cups long-grain white rice
- 2 tablespoons extra-virgin olive oil
- 2 celery stalks with leaves, diced
- 1 green bell pepper, diced
- 1 red bell pepper, diced
- 1–2 fresh red or green chiles, seeded (optional) and diced
- ½ onion, diced
- 4 garlic cloves, minced
- 2 cups shrimp broth or bottled clam juice
- 2 cups chicken or vegetable broth (see page 62 or 61)
- 1 tablespoon chopped fresh thyme, or 1 teaspoon dried
- ¼ teaspoon ground white pepper, or to taste
- ¼ teaspoon freshly ground black pepper, or to taste
- 3 bay leaves
- 1 teaspoon hot pepper sauce, or to taste
- 1 pound shrimp, peeled
- 4 scallions (white and tender green parts), chopped
- ½ cup chopped fresh parsley

CAJUN MACQUE CHOUX

SERVES 3 OR 4

This is a luxurious Cajun specialty of creamed corn, made rich with bacon and shrimp. The fresh tomatoes and basil give it a summery accent, while the chile and black and white pepper contribute heat. Cream is traditional, but evaporated skim milk will lighten the dish considerably.

1 Cut the corn kernels from the cobs. You should have about 4 cups. Use a dull knife to scrape the cobs to extract as much "milk" as possible. Set aside.

2 Cook the bacon over medium heat in a large skillet until crisp, 5 to 8 minutes. Remove the bacon with tongs or a fork and drain on paper towels. Reserve 2 tablespoons of the bacon fat and discard the rest.

3 Return the skillet to medium-high heat. Add the onion, green and red bell peppers, and chile and sauté until limp, about 3 minutes.

4 Add the corn and tomatoes. Stir in enough cream to make a creamy sauce. Stir in the basil, thyme, and black and white pepper. Add sugar, if desired (you want the dish to be rather sweet), and salt to taste. Cover, reduce the heat to medium, and simmer for 10 minutes.

5 Stir in the shrimp. Replace the cover and simmer until the shrimp are pink and firm, about 5 minutes. Stir in the scallions and parsley. Crumble the bacon and mix in. Serve at once.

5–6 ears corn, husked

2 strips bacon

1 onion, diced

1 green bell pepper, diced

1 red bell pepper, diced

1 chile, seeded and diced

4 plum tomatoes, seeded and diced

½–¾ cup light cream, half-and-half, or evaporated skim milk

2 tablespoons chopped fresh basil

2 teaspoons fresh thyme, or 1 teaspoon dried

¼ teaspoon freshly ground black pepper

¼ teaspoon ground white pepper

1–2 teaspoons sugar (optional)

Salt

1 pound shrimp, peeled

2 scallions (white and tender green parts), chopped

2 tablespoons chopped fresh parsley

SAFFRON SHRIMP WITH POTATOES & SPINACH

SERVES 4

When fresh spinach is in season, this tasty combination of shrimp, potatoes, and spinach in a tomato-wine sauce is satisfying and quick to make.

1 Combine the potatoes with salted water to cover in a medium saucepan. Bring to a boil. Continue to boil for about 5 minutes, until almost tender, and drain. Set aside.

2 Combine the wine, tomato paste, and saffron. Set aside.

3 Heat the oil in a large skillet over low heat. Sauté the garlic and red pepper flakes in the oil for about 3 minutes, until fragrant. Stir in the wine mixture, increase the heat to medium-high, and bring to a boil. Add the potatoes and boil for about 3 minutes, or until the sauce is reduced by half and the potatoes are fully tender.

4 Add the shrimp and simmer for about 5 minutes, until the shrimp are pink and cooked through.

5 Carefully stir in the spinach and cook, stirring constantly, until the spinach is wilted, about 1 minute. Season to taste with salt and pepper and serve at once.

1½	pounds new potatoes, quartered or cut into eighths
1½	cups dry white wine
2	tablespoons tomato paste
¼	teaspoon crushed saffron threads
1	tablespoon extra-virgin olive oil
8	large cloves garlic, minced
¼	teaspoon crushed red pepper flakes
1	pound shrimp, peeled
1	pound fresh spinach, trimmed and chopped
	Salt and freshly ground black pepper

LEMONY BLUEFISH WITH POTATOES & ZUCCHINI

SERVES 4 OR 5

Lemon and garlic are all that is needed to highlight the rich flavors of bluefish. Have everything chopped and ready to go before you start cooking and plan to serve as soon as possible. A loaf of bread and a rustic red wine make good accompaniments. If bluefish is unavailable, substitute mackerel.

1 Combine the potatoes with salted water to cover in a medium saucepan. Bring to a boil. Continue to boil for about 5 minutes, until the potatoes are almost tender, and drain.

2 Return the potatoes to the saucepan and toss with the oil, garlic, and shallot.

3 Heat a large skillet over medium-high heat. Sauté the potatoes until they are nicely browned, about 5 minutes. Add the bluefish and zucchini and sauté until the bluefish is cooked through, 3 to 4 minutes.

4 Remove from the heat and add the lemon juice, parsley, and salt and pepper to taste. Toss well. Serve at once.

1½ pounds new potatoes, quartered or cut into eighths

1 tablespoon extra-virgin olive oil

4 cloves garlic, minced

1 shallot, minced

1 pound bluefish fillets, cut into bite-size chunks

2 medium zucchini (1 pound), quartered and sliced

Juice of 2 lemons (4–6 tablespoons)

½ cup chopped fresh parsley

Salt and freshly ground black pepper

SPANISH FISH & POTATO SAUTÉ

SERVES 4

Everyone needs at least one all-purpose, absolutely delicious fish recipe for whipping up on the spur of the moment. This one fits the bill. It is made with canned tomatoes, saffron, potatoes, and peppers — ingredients likely to be found on hand. This version calls for swordfish, but anything that looks good at the market, including shellfish, can be substituted; just adjust the cooking time accordingly.

1 Combine the potatoes with salted water to cover in a medium saucepan. Bring to a boil. Continue to boil for about 5 minutes, until the potatoes are almost tender, and drain. Set aside.

2 Toast the saffron in a small dry skillet over medium heat for 2 to 3 minutes, until fragrant. Set aside.

3 Heat the oil in a large skillet over medium-high heat. Sauté the red and green bell peppers, onion, and garlic in the oil until the peppers are lightly browned, about 5 minutes. Add the tomatoes and toasted saffron and simmer for 1 minute.

4 Add the fish and boiled potatoes to the skillet. Season generously with salt and pepper, cover, and let cook until the fish and potatoes are cooked through, about 8 minutes.

5 Taste and adjust the seasonings. Stir in the parsley and serve immediately.

1 pound new potatoes, quartered or cut into eighths

⅛–¼ teaspoon crushed saffron threads

2 tablespoons extra-virgin olive oil

2 red bell peppers, cubed

1 green bell pepper, cubed

1 onion, halved and cut into slivers

4 garlic cloves, minced

1 can (15 ounces) diced tomatoes with juice

1½ pounds swordfish or other firm, fresh fish, cut into bite-size cubes

Salt and freshly ground black pepper

1 cup chopped fresh parsley

ARROZ CON POLLO

SERVES 4 OR 5

Arroz con pollo — rice with chicken — is a classic combination with an infinite number of variations. Recipes for the dish reach as far back as medieval Spain and can be as contemporary as your neighbor's second-generation adapted version from Puerto Rico. This version is Cuban in inspiration. The olives are what make it distinctive.

1 Wash the rice in at least two changes of water. Drain and set aside.

2 Combine the broth, sherry, and saffron and set aside.

3 Heat the oil in a large skillet over medium-high heat. Sauté the chicken in the oil for 2 minutes. Add the onion, bell pepper, and garlic. Sauté until the vegetables are limp and the chicken is white and firm, 6 to 8 minutes. Add the rice and sauté for another 3 to 5 minutes, until the rice appears opaque.

4 Stir in the broth mixture and bring to a boil. Cover, reduce the heat to maintain a gentle boil, and cook until the liquid is absorbed, about 15 minutes.

5 When the rice is cooked, fluff with a fork. Stir in the tomatoes, peas, and olives. Cover and cook over low heat for 3 minutes, until the peas are cooked through. Season to taste with salt and pepper. Serve at once.

2 cups long-grain white rice

2½ cups chicken broth (see page 62)

½ cup dry sherry

¼ teaspoon crushed saffron threads

2 tablespoons extra-virgin olive oil

1 pound boneless, skinless chicken breasts, cut into bite-size pieces

1 onion, diced

1 green bell pepper, diced

3 cloves garlic, minced

4 tomatoes, seeded and diced, or 2 cups canned diced tomatoes, drained

1 cup frozen peas

10 pimiento-stuffed green olives, sliced (¼ cup)

Salt and freshly ground black pepper

CURRIED CHICKEN & BROCCOLI PILAF

SERVES 4

Use this recipe as a template for a variety of ingredients — turkey can replace the chicken, and asparagus, green beans, or cauliflower can substitute for the broccoli.

1 Wash the rice in at least two changes of water. Drain and set aside.

2 Heat the oil in a large skillet over low heat. Sauté the onion, ginger, garlic, curry powder, cumin, turmeric, cardamom, and cinnamon in the oil for about 5 minutes, until the onion is softened.

3 Stir in the chicken and rice, increase the heat to medium, and sauté for about 5 minutes, until the rice appears opaque.

4 Stir in the broth, water, and salt. Bring to a boil, cover, reduce the heat to maintain a gentle boil, and cook for about 15 minutes, until the liquid is absorbed.

5 While the rice cooks, blanch the broccoli in boiling water to cover for 1 minute. Drain and set aside.

6 When the rice is cooked, fluff with a fork. Stir in the blanched broccoli, raisins, and scallions. Taste and add more salt, if needed. Serve at once.

- 2 cups long-grain rice
- 2 tablespoons canola oil
- 1 onion, finely chopped
- 1 piece fresh ginger (½-inch long), peeled and minced
- 1 garlic clove, minced
- 1 teaspoon curry powder
- ½ teaspoon ground cumin
- ½ teaspoon ground turmeric
- ⅛ teaspoon ground cardamom
- ⅛ teaspoon ground cinnamon
- 1 pound boneless, skinless chicken breasts, diced
- 2 cups chicken broth (see page 62)
- 2 cups water
- ½ teaspoon salt
- 1 large stalk broccoli including florets, chopped
- ½ cup raisins
- 4 scallions (white and tender green parts), chopped

PERFECT SKILLET RICE

It isn't at all difficult to cook rice well, but it does require attention to details. One detail that is often overlooked is washing rice. This step removes excess starch, which tends to make the rice gummy. Washing also removes some of the vitamins and minerals that have been sprayed onto the rice, but the loss is fairly minor. Do not wash rice for risotto; the starch on the surface of the rice contributes to the creamy texture you are trying to achieve.

To wash the rice, place it in a sieve and set the sieve in a bowl of cold water. Swish the rice around with your hands or a spoon until you see the water turn milky white. Drain the rice and repeat the process. Then drain the rice again.

Next toast the rice by tossing with the seasonings in a skillet over medium-high heat until the grains appear dry, opaque, and white; this usually takes 3 to 5 minutes. Stir in the liquid, cover, and bring to a boil. Reduce the heat to maintain a gentle boil. If the pot is not tightly covered, the recipe will not provide enough liquid, and the rice will be slightly hard. If you cook the rice too fast, it will boil over the sides of the skillet and make a mess. Furthermore, you may lose too much liquid and the rice will not cook properly. On the other hand, if you cook it too slowly, the rice will be mushy. Check the rice after 12 minutes. It is done when the liquid is all absorbed and steam holes appear on the surface. The rice should be firm, not sticky or gummy (which indicates overcooking). If the rice is almost, but not quite, done, remove it from the heat and let it sit, covered, for about 3 minutes longer. Then remove the cover and fluff with a fork.

If you plan to hold the rice for more than a few minutes before serving, dry the lid to remove any condensation. Crumple a dishtowel or paper towel and place it on top of the rice before setting the lid back on the pot. This will prevent steam from condensing on the lid and falling back on the rice, making it mushy.

COCK-A-LEEKIE SKILLET POTPIE

SERVES 4 OR 5

Chicken, leeks, and fresh dill make a fragrant filling for a potpie. The generous amount of pastry dough allows for an attractive edging on the crust, as well as for cutouts placed on top. To save time, use refrigerated pie dough instead of making your own.

1 To prepare the crust, combine the flour and salt in a medium mixing bowl. Cut in the butter with a pastry blender or two knives until the mixture resembles coarse crumbs. Add 5 tablespoons ice water to moisten the dough. Lightly mix together to form a ball. If the mixture won't hold together, add additional water, a few drops at a time, until it does. Flatten into a disk. Cover and refrigerate while you prepare the filling.

2 To make the filling, boil the potatoes in salted water to cover until just tender, about 5 minutes. Drain and set aside.

3 Heat the oil over medium-high heat in a large oven-proof skillet. Sauté the chicken and leeks in the oil until the chicken is white and firm, 6 to 8 minutes. Stir in the carrots, peas, bell pepper, and potatoes.

4 Stir together 2 tablespoons of the broth and the cornstarch in a small bowl until you have a smooth paste. Set aside. Add the remaining broth to the skillet and bring to a boil. Stir in the cornstarch mixture. Return to a boil and cook for about 1 minute, until the mixture thickens and clears. Remove from the heat. Stir in 1 tablespoon of the dill. Season to taste with salt and pepper; add more dill, if desired.

CRUST

1½ cups unbleached all-purpose flour

½ teaspoon salt

5 tablespoons butter

5–7 tablespoons ice water

Milk

FILLING

1 pound potatoes, peeled and diced

1 tablespoon canola oil

¾ pound boneless, skinless chicken breast, cubed

2–3 leeks, trimmed and sliced (3 cups)

2 carrots, diced

1 cup frozen peas

½ red bell pepper, diced

1¾ cups chicken broth (see page 62)

2 tablespoons cornstarch

1–2 tablespoons chopped fresh dill

Salt and freshly ground black pepper

5 Preheat the oven to 425°F.

6 On a lightly floured surface, roll out the dough to form a circle at least 2 inches larger than the skillet. Cut out a circle at least 1 inch larger than the skillet. Fit the pastry over the filling in the skillet. Turn under excess dough and flute the edges. Form excess dough into a ball, roll flat and use cookie cutters to make decorative cutouts. Moisten with milk and firmly attach to the crust. Cut holes in the crust for steam to escape.

7 Bake for 25 to 35 minutes, or until the crust is golden brown. Let stand for about 10 minutes before serving.

COOKING REALLY ISN'T ROCKET SCIENCE

Most of my recipes call for using one whole onion or one green bell pepper. One medium onion, diced, generally measures ½ cup. But what if your onion is larger, or smaller? It really doesn't matter. Any resulting flavor differences will be barely perceptible. Don't carefully measure out the cups when it comes to dicing up flavorful vegetables such as onions, peppers, carrots, and celery. Use the whole thing. Don't clutter up your refrigerator with odds and ends. Relax and enjoy the final results of your efforts — cooking really isn't about careful measuring. Baking — cakes and cookies and pastries — that's an entirely different matter.

CHICKEN PAELLA

SERVES 4

Saffron rice with any number of combinations of seafood, chicken, sausage, or rabbit meat is enjoyed throughout Spain. This version gets its flavor from chicken and smoked turkey sausage. The yellow rice, accented with red tomatoes, peppers, and green peas, makes a dazzling feast for the eyes as well as for the palate. For a special supper whipped up in under an hour, this recipe can't be beat.

1 Toast the saffron in a dry skillet over medium heat for 2 to 3 minutes, until fragrant. Add to the broth. Set aside.

2 Heat the oil over medium-high heat in a large skillet. Cook the chicken in the oil until white and firm, 6 to 8 minutes. Remove from the skillet with a slotted spoon. Set aside.

3 Add the sausage to the oil remaining in the skillet and sauté over medium-high heat for 1 minute. Add the onion, bell pepper, and rice. Reduce the heat to medium and sauté until the rice appears opaque and the onion is softened, 3 to 5 minutes.

4 Return the chicken to the skillet, add the broth mixture, and stir well. Cover and bring to a boil. Reduce the heat to maintain a gentle boil and cook until the liquid is absorbed and the rice is tender, about 15 minutes.

5 Fluff the rice with a fork. Carefully stir in the artichoke hearts, peas, and tomato. Season to taste with salt and pepper. Cook for another 3 to 4 minutes, until heated through.

6 Serve immediately.

¼ teaspoon crushed saffron threads

4 cups chicken broth (see page 62)

2 tablespoons extra-virgin olive oil

¾ pound boneless, skinless chicken breast, cut into ¼- by 1-inch strips

¼ pound smoked turkey sausage, sliced ½-inch thick

1 onion, diced

½ red bell pepper, diced

2 cups medium-grain white rice

1 can (14 ounces) artichoke hearts, drained and quartered

1 cup frozen green peas

1 tomato, seeded and diced, or ½ cup canned diced tomatoes, drained

Salt and freshly ground black pepper

CHICKEN & SUMMER VEGETABLE SAUTÉ

SERVES 4

When the garden is producing its summer bounty, a simple combination of chicken and vegetables is very satisfying. Serve with French bread.

1 Bring a large pot of salted water to a boil. Add the green beans and boil for 1 minute. Plunge into cold water to stop the cooking. Drain well and set aside.

2 Heat the oil over medium-high heat in a large skillet. Sauté the chicken in the oil for 6 to 8 minutes, until the chicken is no longer pink and slightly browned outside. Add the beans and garlic and sauté for 1 minute. Add the tomatoes and squash and sauté for 2 to 3 minutes, until the squash is tender.

3 Mix in the herbs, capers, and lemon juice. Season generously with salt and pepper. Serve hot.

½ pound green beans, trimmed and cut into 1-inch pieces

2 tablespoons extra-virgin olive oil

1 pound boneless skinless chicken breasts, cut into bite-size pieces

3–4 cloves garlic, minced

4 tomatoes, seeded and diced

1 yellow summer squash or zucchini, diced

1 tablespoon chopped fresh herbs (basil, oregano, thyme, alone or in any combination)

1 tablespoon capers

2 tablespoons fresh lemon juice, or to taste

Salt and freshly ground black pepper

ONE-DISH TIP:
CAST IRON vs. NONSTICK

Cast-iron skillets will last forever. Once seasoned properly, food will never stick to a cast-iron skillet. If it should lose its seasoning, it is easily reseasoned. Nonstick cookware lasts longer than it used to, but the coatings do eventually wear off. To prolong the life of nonstick cookware, use only plastic or wooden utensils with them. Soak in warm water to loosen any burned-on bits of food, rather than scouring.

LEMONY CHICKEN WITH ARTICHOKES & POTATOES

SERVES 4

Crisp, thyme-flavored potatoes provide the right contrast to the lemony chicken. Oven-roasting them renders them deliciously crusty with a minimum of oil and fuss.

1. To prepare the potatoes, preheat the oven to 425°F. Lightly oil a large sheet pan. Combine the potatoes, oil, garlic, thyme, and salt and pepper to taste in a bowl. Toss well. Spread out the potatoes on the sheet pan in a single layer. Roast for 25 minutes, until browned all over, shaking the pan occasionally for even cooking. Set aside.

2. To prepare the chicken and artichokes, heat the oil in a large skillet over medium-high heat. Sauté the chicken in the oil until white and firm, 6 to 8 minutes. Season to taste with salt and pepper.

3. Add the artichoke hearts, chicken broth, and lemon juice to the skillet. Cook until the liquid in the pan reduces and is slightly thickened, about 2 minutes.

4. Mix in the potatoes. Garnish with the parsley and olives. Serve at once.

POTATOES

- 1½ pounds new potatoes, quartered or cut into eighths
- 2 tablespoons extra-virgin olive oil
- 3 garlic cloves, minced
- 2 teaspoons fresh thyme leaves, or 1 teaspoon dried

  Salt and freshly ground black pepper

CHICKEN AND ARTICHOKES

- 2 tablespoons extra-virgin olive oil
- 1 pound boneless, skinless chicken breasts, cut into bite-size pieces

  Salt and freshly ground black pepper
- 2 cans (14 ounces each) artichoke hearts, quartered and drained
- ½ cup chicken broth (see page 62)
- 2 tablespoons fresh lemon juice
- ¼ cup chopped fresh parsley
- ½ cup pitted, brine-cured black olives, such as kalamata, chopped

CHICKEN & SPINACH WITH WHITE BEANS

SERVES 4

The sunny flavors of tomatoes, rosemary, and olives provide a delicious backdrop to the chicken and spinach. This dish is best served as soon as it is ready; if you must prepare it ahead, make the chicken and sauce and add the spinach at the last minute. Serve with a crusty loaf of fresh bread for sopping up the sauce.

1 Heat the oil in a large skillet over medium-high heat. Sauté the chicken in the oil until white and firm, 6 to 8 minutes. Remove from the skillet and keep warm.

2 Reduce the heat to medium. Add the celery, garlic, and shallots to the skillet and sauté until the vegetables are limp and fragrant, about 5 minutes. Add the tomatoes and rosemary and simmer for 3 minutes.

3 Dissolve the cornstarch in the chicken broth and add to the skillet. Bring to a boil and cook until the sauce is thickened, about 1 minute. Add the beans and cooked chicken and continue to cook until heated through, about 3 minutes.

4 Carefully stir in the spinach and cook until wilted, about 3 minutes. Season to taste with salt and pepper.

5 Garnish with the olives. Serve at once.

2 tablespoons extra-virgin olive oil

1½ pounds boneless, skinless chicken breasts, cut into bite-size pieces

2 celery stalks, minced

4 garlic cloves, minced

2 shallots, minced

1 can (15 ounces) diced tomatoes with juice

1 teaspoon fresh rosemary, or ½ teaspoon dried

1 tablespoon cornstarch

1 cup chicken broth (see page 62)

1 can (15 ounces) cannellini beans, drained and rinsed

12 ounces fresh spinach, trimmed and chopped

Salt and freshly ground black pepper

½ cup pitted, brine-cured black olives, such as kalamata, chopped

TURKEY WITH WINTER VEGETABLES

SERVES 4

Here is a delicious feast with aromatic vegetables. Be sure to serve with a loaf of French bread to mop up the tasty sauce. Use cranberry sauce as an accompaniment for a festive touch. To use leftover turkey in this dish, simply add it to the vegetables along with the cooked potatoes and rutabagas.

1 Combine the potatoes and rutabaga in a saucepan with water to cover. Cover and bring to a boil. Boil for 5 to 8 minutes, until tender. Drain and set aside.

2 Heat the oil in a large skillet over medium-high heat. Sauté the turkey in the oil for 2 minutes. Add the leeks, carrots, and garlic, and sauté for 3 minutes. Add the cooked potatoes and rutabaga and the broth and thyme. Simmer for 5 minutes.

3 Add the cornstarch mixture and simmer for 5 minutes more, or until the turkey is cooked through and the sauce is thickened. Season to taste with salt and pepper. Sprinkle with the parsley and serve.

2 medium potatoes, peeled and cubed

1 rutabaga, peeled and cubed

2 tablespoons extra-virgin olive oil

2/3 pound boneless, skinless turkey thigh, cut into bite-size cubes

2 leeks, trimmed and sliced

2 carrots, cubed

2 garlic cloves, minced

2 cups chicken broth (see page 62)

1 teaspoon chopped fresh thyme, or 1/2 teaspoon dried

1 1/2 tablespoons cornstarch dissolved in 1/4 cup water

Salt and freshly ground black pepper

1/4 cup chopped fresh parsley

JAMBALAYA

SERVES 4 OR 5

This Cajun classic combines ham, rice, and vegetables — a terrifically flavorful one-dish meal.

1 Wash the rice in at least two changes of water. Drain and set aside.

2 Cook the bacon over medium heat in a large skillet until crisp, 5 to 8 minutes. Transfer the bacon with tongs to paper towels to drain.

3 Return the skillet to medium-high heat. Add the okra, bell pepper, onion, and garlic, and sauté for 3 to 4 minutes, until the vegetables are limp.

4 Add the rice to the skillet and sauté until the rice appears opaque, 3 to 4 minutes. Stir in the broth, tomatoes, and hot pepper sauce. Cover and bring to a boil. Reduce the heat to maintain a gentle boil and cook until the liquid is absorbed, about 15 minutes.

5 Fluff the rice with a fork. Mix in the ham and parsley. Crumble the bacon and mix in. Season to taste with salt and pepper, and more hot sauce if desired. Serve hot.

2 cups long-grain white rice

2 slices bacon

½ pound okra, trimmed and sliced ¼-inch thick

1 green bell pepper, diced

1 onion, diced

3 garlic cloves, minced

4 cups chicken broth (see page 62)

1 can (15 ounces) diced tomatoes with juice

2 dashes hot pepper sauce, or more to taste

½ pound smoked ham or turkey breast, diced

¼ cup chopped fresh parsley

Salt and freshly ground black pepper

ORIGINS OF JAMBALAYA

Two popularly told stories explain how this Cajun classic got its name. The most repeated holds that the name derives from the French word for ham — *jambon* (most recipes for jambalaya require ham). A more colorful version of the tale describes a gentleman arriving late and hungry at a Louisiana inn. He orders the innkeeper, a man by the name of Jean, to *balayez*, the French word for "mix together." The innkeeper combines rice, meats, and vegetables, and the guest proclaims the dish delicious, calling it "Jean Balayez."

SKILLET LASAGNA

SERVES 5

Each bite in this quick-to-prepare mixed-up skillet version of lasagna provides the flavors of the original.

1 Bring a pot of salted water to a boil. Cook the pasta in the water until just barely done; do not overcook. The pasta should still be firm. Drain and set aside.

2 Brown the sausage in a large skillet over medium-high heat, about 3 minutes. Add the onion and bell pepper and sauté for 3 minutes. Add the zucchini and garlic and sauté for another minute. Drain off any excess fat.

3 Stir in the tomato sauce, oregano, basil, and thyme. Season to taste with salt and pepper. Simmer for 10 minutes. Stir again and adjust the seasonings.

4 Meanwhile, mix together the ricotta, mozzarella, Parmesan, parsley, egg, and ¼ teaspoon black pepper in a medium bowl.

5 Stir the pasta and ricotta mixture into the skillet. Cover and simmer for 15 minutes, stirring occasionally. Let stand for 5 minutes before serving.

14 ounces flat pasta, such as farfalle

¾ pound Italian sausage (sweet or hot), casings removed

1 onion, finely chopped

1 green bell pepper, finely chopped

1 medium-sized zucchini, diced

4 garlic cloves, minced

1 can (28 ounces) unseasoned tomato sauce

4 teaspoons dried oregano

1 teaspoon dried basil

½ teaspoon dried thyme
   Salt and freshly ground black pepper

1 cup ricotta cheese

2 ounces mozzarella, grated (½ cup)

¼ cup freshly grated Parmesan

¼ cup chopped fresh parsley

1 egg, lightly beaten

¼ teaspoon black pepper

SAUSAGE & KALE WITH GARLIC ROASTED POTATOES

SERVES 4

Kale was once barely known in the United States, though it has long been a popular green in Germany, the Netherlands, and Scotland because it grows best in northern climates. This is a hearty dish that can be enjoyed no matter where you live.

1 Preheat the oven to 425°F. Lightly grease a large baking sheet with oil.

2 Combine the potatoes, 2 tablespoons of the oil, garlic, oregano, and salt and pepper to taste in a medium bowl and toss to coat. Spread out in a single layer on the baking sheet and roast for about 25 minutes, until browned and tender.

3 Heat the remaining 1 tablespoon oil in a large skillet. Sauté the sausage and onion in the oil until the sausage is mostly browned, 4 to 6 minutes.

4 Stir in half the kale and all the broth. Cook, stirring, until the kale is wilted. Stir in the remaining kale. Cover and simmer for about 5 minutes, until the kale is wilted and tender but still bright green.

5 Mix in the beans, then the potatoes, Season with salt and pepper and serve at once.

1½ pounds red potatoes, quartered or cut into eighths

3 tablespoons extra-virgin olive oil

3 garlic cloves, minced

1 teaspoon dried oregano

Salt and freshly ground black pepper

½ pound sweet or hot Italian sausage, sliced 1 inch thick

1 onion, halved and slivered

8 cups chopped fresh kale, tough stems discarded

1½ cups chicken broth (see page 62)

1 can (15 ounces) cannellini beans, rinsed and drained

SAUTÉED PORK & PEPPERS WITH WHITE BEANS

SERVES 4

The flavors of the Southwest — peppers, tomatoes, cumin — combine with pork and white beans to make a meal in minutes. Don't forget the bread — you'll want to wipe your bowl clean.

1 Heat the oil with the cumin over medium-high heat in a large skillet. Add the pork, sprinkle with salt and pepper, and sauté for 3 to 4 minutes, until the pork is browned.

2 Add the onion and bell peppers and sauté for 2 minutes. Add the zucchini and garlic and sauté for 1 minute. Add the beans, tomatoes, and chiles. Reduce the heat and simmer for 5 minutes.

3 Taste and add more salt and pepper, if desired. Stir in the cilantro and scallions. Serve at once.

- 1 tablespoon extra-virgin olive oil
- 1½ teaspoons ground cumin
- ¾ pound pork tenderloin, cut into ¼ by 1-inch strips

  Salt and freshly ground black pepper
- 1 onion, halved lengthwise and slivered
- 1 large green bell pepper, julienned
- 1 large red bell pepper, julienned
- 1 medium-sized zucchini, julienned
- 3 garlic cloves
- 1 can (15 ounces) cannellini beans, drained and rinsed
- 1 can (15 ounces) diced tomatoes with juice
- 1 can (4 ounces) chopped green chiles, drained
- ¼ cup chopped fresh cilantro or parsley
- 2 scallions (white and tender green parts), chopped

SKILLET SHEPHERD'S PIE

SERVES 4 OR 5

In the north of England and Scotland, where Sunday's roast was mutton or lamb, Monday's supper of leftovers was often a "shepherd's pie" — a dish of chopped-up leftover roast, gravy, and vegetables with a topping of mashed potatoes, or sometimes pastry. It's rare that any of us have leftover mutton, but a shepherd's pie remains a homey favorite. Topped with buttermilk mashed potatoes, this version gives you a choice of ground lamb, beef, or turkey and tucks in plenty of vegetables.

1 Combine the potatoes with salted water to cover in a medium saucepan and bring to a boil. Boil until tender, 10 to 15 minutes. Drain and set aside.

2 Heat the oil in a large ovenproof skillet over medium-high heat. Sauté the lamb in the oil until the lamb is mostly browned, about 5 minutes. Add the leek and carrot and sauté for 2 to 3 minutes, until the leek is limp. Add the zucchini and garlic and sauté for another minute. Stir in the corn and reduce the heat to low.

3 Mix together the broth, tomato paste, cornstarch, rosemary, and thyme in a small bowl. Stir into the skillet. Increase the heat to medium-high and cook, stirring frequently, until the mixture thickens, 1 to 2 minutes. Cook for another minute, then remove from the heat. Season to taste with salt and pepper.

4 Preheat the broiler.

5 Rice or mash the cooked potatoes in a medium bowl. Whip in the buttermilk and butter. Season to taste with salt and pepper.

6 Spoon the mashed potatoes over the lamb mixture in the skillet, smoothing the top. Place under the broiler and broil until browned on top, 5 to 8 minutes. Let stand for 5 minutes before serving.

1½ pounds baking potatoes, peeled and sliced

1 tablespoon extra-virgin olive oil

1 pound ground lamb, beef, or turkey

1 leek, trimmed and sliced

1 carrot, diced

1 medium-sized zucchini, diced

3 cloves garlic, minced

1 cup fresh or frozen corn kernels

1 cup beef broth or chicken broth (see page 62)

1 tablespoon tomato paste

1 tablespoon cornstarch

½ teaspoon dried rosemary

½ teaspoon dried thyme

Salt and freshly ground black pepper

1 cup buttermilk

1 tablespoon butter

TAMALE PIE

SERVES 4

The original tamale pies were made with a ground meat filling and a topping of cornmeal mush. In this version, fragrant, cumin-scented chili and corn-rich cornbread combine in one skillet. The chili is fairly mild — jazz it up with more chili powder or ground chiles if you prefer.

1 Preheat the oven to 425°F.

2 To prepare the chili filling, heat the oil in a large skillet over medium-high heat. Sauté the beef, onion, bell pepper, chili powder, and cumin in the oil until the meat is browned, 6 to 8 minutes. Drain off any liquid.

3 Add the tomato sauce and beans. Season to taste with salt and pepper and ground chile; add more chili powder if desired.

4 Spread the cheese over the chili.

5 To prepare the cornmeal topping, combine the corn, buttermilk, and oil in a blender and process until fairly smooth. Blend in the egg.

6 Mix together the cornmeal, flour, sugar, baking powder, and salt in a medium bowl. Pour in the buttermilk mixture and stir just until moistened. The batter will be lumpy. Spread the batter over the chili mixture in the skillet.

7 Bake for 20 to 30 minutes, until the topping is golden and firm. (Batter made with frozen corn will take longer to bake than batter made with fresh corn.)

8 Let stand for 5 minutes before serving.

CHILI FILLING

1 tablespoon extra-virgin olive oil

1 pound ground beef or ground pork

1 onion, diced

1 green bell pepper, diced

1 tablespoon chili powder

1 teaspoon ground cumin

1 can (15 ounces) unseasoned tomato sauce

1 can (15 ounces) kidney beans, pink beans, or pinto beans, drained and rinsed

Salt and freshly ground black pepper

Ground chile, such as ancho, chipotle, or New Mexico

¼ pound Monterey Jack, shredded (1 cup)

CORNMEAL TOPPING

2 cups fresh or frozen corn kernels

¾ cup buttermilk

¼ cup canola oil

1 egg

1 cup yellow cornmeal

¾ cup unbleached all-purpose flour

3 tablespoons sugar

2 teaspoons baking powder

1 teaspoon salt

CHILI MAC

SERVES 6

Is this a variation on Cincinnati chili? More likely it is a fast recipe that first appeared on the back of a box of macaroni, which then spawned dozens of variations, including General Mills Hamburger Helper, introduced in 1970. This recipe couldn't be faster, easier, or more family-friendly.

1 Heat the oil in a large skillet over medium heat. Cook the beef, onion, green pepper, jalapeños, garlic, chili powder, cumin, and salt in the oil, stirring frequently, until the meat is browned, about 15 minutes. Drain off any liquid.

2 Stir in the tomatoes, beans, and water. Increase the heat and bring to a boil. Stir in the macaroni, cover the pan, and simmer over medium-low heat for 15 to 20 minutes, stirring frequently, until the macaroni is tender.

3 Stir in the corn and season generously with pepper. Taste and adjust the seasonings. Simmer until the corn is heated through, about 5 minutes. Serve hot, passing the cheese at the table.

- 1 tablespoon extra-virgin olive oil
- 1 pound ground beef or ground turkey
- 1 large onion, diced
- 1 large green bell pepper, diced
- 1–2 jalapeños, seeded and diced
- 2 garlic cloves, minced
- ¼ cup chili powder
- ½ teaspoon ground cumin
- 1½ teaspoons salt, or to taste
- 1 can (28 ounces) crushed tomatoes
- 1 can (15 ounces) kidney beans, rinsed and drained
- 1½ cups water
- 2 cups uncooked elbow macaroni
- 1½ cups fresh or frozen corn kernels
  Freshly ground black pepper
  Freshly grated Cheddar or Monterey Jack, to serve

STOVETOP MAC 'N' CHEESE WITH HAM & PEAS

SERVES 4 TO 6

Whether you make it in a skillet or pasta pot, this is such an easy, fast recipe, it deserves its place in a book devoted to one-dish meals. This is one of the best ways to use leftover ham. But if you don't have the ham, or the peas for that matter, the dish is still worth considering, because this macaroni and cheese is as quick to make as the boxed kind, but so much better in flavor.

1 Bring a large pot of salted water to a boil; cook the macaroni until just done, about 8 minutes. Drain and return to the pot.

2 Put the pot over the lowest possible heat and add the butter, cheese, mustard, milk, ham, and peas. Stir until the cheese melts. Season to taste with salt and pepper. Serve immediately.

1 pound elbow macaroni

5 tablespoons butter

2½ cups grated sharp Cheddar (about 10 ounces)

1 tablespoon Dijon mustard

½ cup milk

½ pound ham, diced

2 cups frozen peas

Salt and freshly ground black pepper

LAMB & BARLEY WITH WINTER VEGETABLES

SERVES 4

Flavorful lamb and nutty barley make a great pair. The addition of aromatic leeks, turnips, and carrots turn this rustic combination into a satisfying dish. Because barley cooks slowly, this dish takes a little over an hour to prepare. But during the 45 minutes that the barley is cooking, the pot doesn't need tending.

1 Heat the oil in a large skillet over medium-high heat. Sprinkle the lamb with 1 teaspoon of the thyme and season with salt and pepper. Sauté in the oil until well browned, about 5 minutes. Remove the lamb with a slotted spoon and set aside.

2 Add the leeks, carrot, and turnip to the skillet and sauté for about 3 minutes, until softened. Add the barley and sauté for 1 minute. Add the boiling water, 1 teaspoon salt, remaining thyme, and the browned lamb. Stir well. Cover, reduce the heat, and simmer until the liquid is absorbed, about 45 minutes.

3 Fluff with a fork before serving.

2 tablespoons extra-virgin olive oil

1 pound lamb (from leg), cut into bite-size pieces

1½ teaspoons dried thyme

Salt and freshly ground black pepper

3 leeks, trimmed and sliced

1 carrot, diced

1 turnip or 1 small rutabaga, peeled and diced

1½ cups pearl barley

3 cups boiling water

1 teaspoon salt

LAMB COUSCOUS

SERVES 4

Couscous is a staple in the cooking of North Africa, and lamb — or kid — is the meat of choice. Seasonings are bold.

1 Heat the oil in a large skillet over medium-high heat. Sauté the cumin, cinnamon, ground chile, lamb, and onion until the onion is limp, about 3 minutes.

2 Add the bell peppers, carrot, and zucchini and sauté for another 3 minutes, until the lamb is mostly browned and the vegetables are slightly softened.

3 Add the tomatoes, then the broth. Stir in the couscous, cover, and reduce the heat to a gentle simmer. Cook for about 15 minutes, until the couscous is tender. The mixture will still be moist. Season to taste with salt and pepper, and serve immediately.

2 tablespoons extra-virgin olive oil

2 teaspoons ground cumin

½ teaspoon ground cinnamon

½ teaspoon ground chile, such as ancho, cayenne, or New Mexico

1 pound lamb (from leg), cut into bite-size pieces

1 onion, halved lengthwise and slivered

1 green bell pepper, diced

1 red bell pepper, diced

1 carrot, diced

1 medium-sized zucchini, diced

1 can (15 ounces) diced tomatoes with juice

2 cups chicken broth (see page 62)

1 cup couscous

Salt and freshly ground black pepper

OVEN-BAKED SUPPERS

BAKED MACARONI & CHEESE WITH VEGETABLES

SERVES 4 TO 6

Macaroni and cheese without vegetables just isn't a complete meal, so why not add vegetables to this perennial favorite? If different vegetables are preferred — frozen peas or green beans are recommended — just throw them into the pasta water about 2 minutes before the pasta is done. Fresh cauliflower can be substituted for the broccoli.

1 Preheat the oven to 350°F. Lightly grease a large casserole dish with butter.

2 Bring a large pot of salted water to a boil. Add the macaroni and boil. About 3 minutes before the macaroni is done according to the cooking time on the package, add the broccoli. About 1 minute before the macaroni is done, add the carrot. Continue boiling until the macaroni is al dente. Drain well. Transfer to the casserole dish.

3 To make the cheese sauce, melt the butter over medium heat in a medium saucepan. Stir in the flour and dry mustard to form a smooth paste. Stir in the milk and bring to a boil, stirring to prevent lumps. When the sauce thickens, stir in the Cheddar until melted.

4 Stir the sauce into the macaroni and vegetables. Season with salt and pepper.

5 Bake for 30 minutes, until bubbly and browned. Serve hot.

1 pound elbow macaroni

1 head broccoli, broken into florets

1 large carrot, grated

4 tablespoons butter

¼ cup unbleached all-purpose flour

1 teaspoon dry mustard

2 cups milk

1 pound sharp Cheddar, grated
Salt and freshly ground black pepper

MEXICAN LASAGNA

SERVES 4

There are as many names for this dish as there are recipes. In Mexico, this dish would probably be called *budin Azteca*, or Aztec Pie. When the pie crossed the border in Texas, it was readily adapted and made with beef, or chicken, or beans. It may be called Mexican lasagna, stacked enchiladas, tortilla torte, torta tortilla, or Southwestern casserole. By whatever name, the dish is a home-style favorite, with layers of tortillas, salsa, and cheese.

1 Preheat the oven to 425°F.

2 Heat the olive oil in a large nonstick skillet over medium-high heat. Sauté the onion, bell peppers, and chiles until the onion is limp, about 3 minutes. Stir in the tomatoes and simmer for 5 minutes. Remove from the heat. Stir in the cilantro and season to taste with salt and pepper.

3 Heat ½ inch of oil in a medium skillet over medium-high heat. Using tongs, dip tortillas one by one in the oil just long enough to soften, 10 to 15 seconds. Drain on paper towels. (This step is optional, but it improves the flavor and texture of the finished dish — because everything is better fried.) Cut the tortillas into wedges.

4 Spoon about ½ cup of the tomato mixture into a 1½ quart casserole dish. Arrange an overlapping layer of tortillas wedges on top (use one-third of the tortillas). Spoon 1 cup of the tomato mixture on top. Spread about half of the refried beans in an even layer on top of the tomato layer. Sprinkle with one-quarter of the cheese and half the olives. Cover with another layer of tortillas and tomato mixture. Top with the remaining refried beans, then one-quarter of the cheese and the remaining olives. Arrange a final layer of tortillas on top. Spoon the remaining tomato mixture over this layer. Top with the sour cream and the remaining cheese.

5 Bake for about 25 minutes, until the cheese is melted and the filling is heated through. Let stand for 10 minutes before serving.

2 tablespoons extra-virgin olive oil

1 onion, halved and slivered

1 green bell pepper, julienned

1 red bell pepper, julienned

2 fresh or canned green chiles, seeded and diced

2 cups fresh or canned seeded and diced tomatoes

¼ cup chopped fresh cilantro

Salt and freshly ground black pepper

Oil, for frying (optional)

1 package (9 ounces) corn tortillas

2 cups homemade refried beans or 1 can (15 ounces)

2 cups grated Monterey Jack or Cheddar

1 cup sliced California black olives

½ cup sour cream

VEGETABLE LASAGNA

SERVES 6 TO 9

Vegetables replace ground meat in this vegetarian version of lasagna. Of course, there's nothing to stop you from browning a pound of ground meat or sausage with the vegetables for an over-the-top festive lasagna.

1 Heat the oil in a large saucepan over medium-high heat. Sauté the eggplant in the oil until tender, 8 to 10 minutes. Add the bell pepper, onion, zucchini, mushrooms, and garlic. Sauté until the mushrooms give up their juice, 5 to 10 minutes.

2 Add the tomato sauce to the vegetables. Season to taste with the herbs, if using, and salt and pepper.

3 Combine the ricotta, egg, and basil in a medium bowl and mix well.

4 Preheat the oven to 350°F. Lightly grease a 9- by 13-inch baking pan with oil.

5 To assemble the lasagna, spread about 2 cups of the sauce in the prepared baking dish. Place 3 lasagna noodles over the sauce. The noodles should not touch or overlap. Spread a third of the ricotta mixture evenly over the noodles. Top with another 1½ to 2 cups sauce. Sprinkle a quarter of the mozzarella and a quarter of the Parmesan cheese on top. Repeat the layers two more times. Top with the remaining 3 lasagna noodles. Spread the remaining sauce on top. Sprinkle with the remaining cheeses. Cover with foil.

6 Bake the lasagna for 30 minutes. Remove the foil and bake for another 10 to 15 minutes, until bubbly and browned.

7 Let the lasagna stand for 5 minutes before cutting into serving pieces. Serve hot or warm.

3 tablespoons extra-virgin olive oil

1 small to medium-sized eggplant, peeled and diced

1 red or green bell pepper, diced

1 onion, diced

1 zucchini, diced

½ pound button mushrooms, chopped

4 garlic cloves, thinly sliced

6 cups well-seasoned tomato sauce, such as marinara

Chopped fresh herbs (rosemary, thyme, oregano, alone or in any combination) (optional)

Salt and freshly ground black pepper

15–16 ounces (about 1½ cups) ricotta cheese

1 large egg, slightly beaten

2 tablespoons chopped fresh basil

12 no-cook lasagna noodles

4 cups shredded mozzarella cheese

1 cup freshly grated Parmesan

CHICKEN DIVAN

SERVES 4

Here is the dish that gets the credit for introducing broccoli to mainstream America. Before Chicken Divan, broccoli was rarely found outside immigrant Italian communities. This dish was created in the 1930s at the Divan Parisien Restaurant in New York, a restaurant that was once voted the seventh most popular restaurant in the country. From Manhattan, the recipe traveled to more and more dining rooms and was kept alive in community cookbooks long after the restaurant had closed its doors.

1 Bring a large pot of water to a boil. Add the broccoli and blanch for 3 minutes. Drain and immediately plunge into cold water to stop the cooking. Drain well. Transfer the broccoli to a clean towel and pat dry.

2 Preheat the oven to 350°F. Grease a 9- by 13-inch baking dish with butter.

3 Heat 2 tablespoons of the butter and the olive oil in a large skillet over medium-high heat. Season the chicken with the salt and pepper. Place ¾ cup of the flour in a shallow bowl. Dredge the chicken in the flour and add to the skillet in a single layer. Sauté the chicken on both sides until browned, about 4 minutes per side. Remove the skillet from the heat and transfer the chicken to a bowl to keep warm while you prepare the sauce.

4 Return the skillet to medium heat. Add the remaining 1 tablespoon butter and the garlic. Sprinkle in the remaining ¼ cup flour and whisk until smooth. Stir in the broth, milk, and sherry, and bring to a boil. Remove from the heat and stir in ½ cup of the cheese. Season to taste with more salt and pepper.

5 To assemble the casserole, arrange the broccoli in the baking dish. Pour half the sauce over the broccoli. Arrange the chicken on top. Cover with the remaining sauce. Sprinkle the remaining ¼ cup cheese over all.

6 Bake for 30 minutes. Serve hot.

1½ pounds broccoli (3 large heads), chopped

3 tablespoons butter

2 tablespoons extra-virgin olive oil

1–1½ pounds boneless, skinless chicken breast cutlets

Salt and freshly ground black pepper

1 cup unbleached all-purpose flour

2 garlic cloves, minced

1 cup chicken broth (see page 62)

1 cup milk

¼ cup dry sherry

¾ cup grated Gruyère

KING RANCH CHICKEN

SERVES 6

Think "Mexican lasagna" meets chicken à la king, and you get the idea behind this Texas classic.

1 Preheat the oven to 350°F. Lightly grease a 9- by 13-inch baking dish with oil.

2 First, prepare the sauce. Melt the butter in a medium saucepan over medium heat. Sauté the garlic and chili powder in the butter until fragrant, about 1 minute. Stir in the flour until you have a smooth paste. Cook for 1 minute, stirring constantly. Stir in the broth, then the milk, stirring until the mixture is smooth and thick. Remove from the heat and stir in the sour cream. Season to taste with the salt and pepper.

3 To make the filling, heat the oil in a large skillet over medium-high heat. Sauté the bell peppers, onion, chiles, and mushrooms in the oil until the mushrooms give up their juice, about 8 minutes. Stir in the chicken and tomatoes. Season to taste with salt and pepper and remove from the heat.

4 Heat ½ inch of oil in a medium skillet over medium-high heat. Holding the tortillas with tongs, dip them one by one into the oil just long enough to soften, 10 to 15 seconds. Drain on paper towels. (This step is optional, but it improves the flavor and texture of the finished dish — because everything is better fried.)

5 To assemble the casserole, arrange six tortillas in the prepared baking dish. Cover with half the chicken mixture, one-third of the sauce, and one-third of the cheese. Scatter half the olives over the cheese. Repeat the layer with tortillas, chicken, sauce, cheese, and olives. Finish with six more tortillas, the remaining sauce, and the remaining cheese.

6 Bake for about 30 minutes, until browned and bubbly. Let sit for 5 minutes, then serve.

SAUCE

- 6 tablespoons butter
- 2 cloves garlic, minced
- 2 teaspoons chili powder
- 6 tablespoons unbleached all-purpose flour
- 2 cups chicken broth (see page 62)
- 1 cup milk
- ½ cup sour cream
  Salt and freshly ground black pepper

FILLING

- 2 tablespoons extra-virgin olive oil
- 1 red bell pepper, julienned
- 1 green bell pepper, julienned
- 1 onion, halved and sliced
- 2–4 fresh or canned green chiles, seeded (optional) and sliced
- 4 ounces mushrooms, sliced
- 4 cups chopped or shredded cooked chicken
- 1 can (15 ounces) diced tomatoes, drained
  Salt and freshly ground black pepper
  Oil, for frying (optional)
- 18 corn tortillas
- 8 ounces Monterey Jack cheese, grated
- ½ cup chopped pimiento-stuffed green olives

CHICKEN & RICE

SERVES 4 TO 6

Chicken and rice, arroz con pollo, chicken biryani, chicken rice pilaf — there are countless variations on this combination. This particular variation is simply flavored and delicious. The sherry is essential to cut the greasiness of the chicken.

1 Wash the rice in at least two changes of water. Drain and set aside.

2 Preheat the oven to 400°F.

3 Combine the broth, sherry, and thyme, and set aside.

4 Heat the oil in a large skillet over medium-high heat. Season the chicken with the salt and pepper, add enough pieces to fit in the skillet in a single layer, and brown until quite dark, turning several times, about 10 minutes. Remove the chicken and keep warm. Add the remaining chicken and brown. Remove from the skillet. Pour off all but 2 tablespoons fat from the skillet.

5 Lower the heat to medium. Add the mushrooms, onion, and garlic, and sauté until the mushrooms give up their juice, about 5 minutes. Stir the rice and sauté for another 3 to 5 minutes, until the rice appears opaque.

6 Scrape the mixture into a 9- by 13-inch baking dish. Pour in the broth mixture. Arrange the chicken on top of the rice. Cover with aluminum foil.

7 Bake for 55 minutes. Remove the cover and add the peas. Replace the cover and return to the oven for 5 minutes.

8 With a spatula, fluff the rice and mix in the peas. Serve hot.

2 cups long-grain white rice

2½ cups chicken broth (see page 62)

½ cup dry sherry

1 tablespoon chopped fresh thyme

2 tablespoons extra-virgin olive oil

8 bone-in chicken thighs (about 3 pounds)

Salt and freshly ground black pepper

½ pound mushrooms, trimmed and sliced

1 onion, diced

3 cloves garlic, minced

2 cups frozen peas

HERB-ROASTED CHICKEN WITH VEGETABLES

SERVES 4 TO 6

Herbert Hoover did *not* promise a "chicken in every pot," but the Republican National Committee inserted the phrase into ads during Hoover's 1928 campaign. A vote for Hoover, the ad said, would continue the prosperity of the Republican administrations of Harding and Coolidge, which had "reduced hours and increased earning capacity, silenced discontent, put the proverbial 'chicken in every pot,' and a car in every backyard, to boot." One small chicken, stretched with lots of vegetables, fed a family more healthfully than a large chicken and no vegetables.

1 Preheat the oven to 450°F.

2 Rinse the chicken under cold running water and pat dry. Set on a large roasting pan on a rack. (The pan must be large enough to hold the vegetables in a single layer surrounding the chicken.)

3 Combine 3 tablespoons of the oil, the lemon juice, parsley, chopped fresh herbs, 2 teaspoons of the salt, and pepper, to taste in a large bowl. Mix well. Rub the mixture onto the chicken and inside the chicken cavity.

4 Add the potatoes, carrots, beets, rutabaga, shallots, and garlic to the bowl. Add the remaining 2 tablespoons oil and 1 teaspoon salt. Toss gently to coat the vegetables. Arrange the vegetables in a single layer around the chicken.

5 Roast for about 1 hour, until the juices run clear from the chicken and a leg moves easily. Stir the vegetables once or twice during the roasting to promote even roasting.

6 Let the chicken sit for 10 minutes. Transfer to a serving platter. Turn the vegetables in the pan juices. Taste and add salt and pepper, if desired. Spoon the vegetables around the chicken. Serve immediately.

---

1 whole chicken, 3½–5 pounds, giblets and neck removed

5 tablespoons extra-virgin olive oil
   Juice of ½ lemon (1–1½ tablespoons)

¼ cup chopped fresh parsley

¼ cup chopped fresh herbs (chervil, lovage, marjoram, oregano, rosemary, sage, savory, thyme, alone or in any combination)

3 teaspoons coarse sea salt or kosher salt
   Freshly ground black pepper

8 red bliss or new potatoes, cut into eighths

3 carrots, sliced ½ inch thick

3 golden or red beets, peeled and sliced ½ inch thick

1 rutabaga, peeled, halved, and sliced ½ inch thick

6 shallots, halved

1 head garlic, cloves separated and peeled

CHICKEN POTPIE

SERVES 6

In the old days, farm wives would slaughter chickens that weren't worth feeding over the winter because their time of good egg production had passed. This Yankee classic was created to take advantage of those old stewing hens. It is also delicious when made with the typical supermarket chicken we find today. Feel free to substitute whatever vegetables you have on hand.

1 Place the chicken in a large pot. Cover with the water. Add the onion, garlic, parsley, and peppercorns. Bring to a boil, then reduce the heat to maintain a slow simmer, and simmer for 1 hour, until the chicken is tender. Turn off the heat and allow the chicken to cool in the cooking liquid.

2 Cover the rutabaga with salted water in a small saucepan and bring to a boil. Boil until just tender, 5 to 8 minutes. Drain.

3 When the chicken is cool enough to handle, remove it from the broth. Discard the skin and bones. Chop the meat into bite-size pieces. Strain the broth and discard the solids. Skim off any fat that rises to the top. Reserve 3 cups broth for the potpie and refrigerator or freeze the remainder for other recipes.

4 Heat the oil in a large saucepan over medium heat. Sauté the leeks in the oil until tender, about 5 minutes. Sprinkle in the flour and stir until all the flour is absorbed into the oil. Whisk in the 3 cups reserved broth and stir until thickened and smooth. Stir in the chicken, rutabaga, carrot, peas, and dill. Season to taste with salt and pepper. Bring to a boil. Keep hot while you prepare the biscuits.

5 Preheat the oven to 450°F. Set out a 9- by 13-inch baking pan.

6 Combine the flour, baking powder, and salt in a food processor. Add the butter and process until the mixture resembles coarse crumbs. Pour in the

4 pounds chicken parts, all white meat, all dark meat, or a mixture of white and dark meat

6–8 cups water

1 onion, quartered

2 garlic cloves, peeled and left whole

1 bunch flat-leaf parsley

1 teaspoon black peppercorns

1 medium-sized rutabaga, peeled and diced

6 tablespoons extra-virgin olive oil

2 medium-sized leeks, trimmed and sliced

6 tablespoons unbleached all-purpose flour

1 carrot, diced

1 cup frozen peas or green beans

1 tablespoon chopped fresh dill, or 1 teaspoon dried thyme

Salt and freshly ground black pepper

buttermilk and process to make a soft dough. Knead a few times on a lightly floured board. Pat out the dough to a thickness of about 1 inch. Cut into 3-inch rounds. By gathering the scraps and patting out again, you should get 12 biscuits.

7 Pour the hot chicken mixture into the baking pan. Place the biscuit rounds on top. Bake for 15 to 18 minutes, until the biscuits are golden and the chicken mixture is bubbling.

8 Let stand for a few minutes before serving.

BISCUIT TOPPING

- 3 cups unbleached all-purpose flour
- 2 tablespoons baking powder
- 1½ teaspoons salt
- ⅔ cup butter, cut into pieces
- 1 cup buttermilk

ONE-DISH TIP:
THE SECRET OF SUCCESS FOR POTPIES

The secret of success when it comes to potpies is to have the filling mixture hot when you place the biscuits on top. If the mixture is cool, the biscuits will be gummy. If you want to prepare the casserole in advance, keep the biscuits and filling in separate containers in the refrigerator. Reheat the filling until bubbly. Transfer to a baking pan and set the cold biscuits on top. Add a few extra minutes to the baking time to compensate for the cold biscuits.

Another option is to bake the biscuits separately (for 15 to 18 minutes at 450°F) and serve alongside the chicken mixture.

CHICKEN TETRAZZINI

SERVES 6

They don't invent dishes like this anymore, and they don't make celebrities out of opera divas as they once did. Chicken Tetrazzini was named after the Florentine Nightingale, Luisa Tetrazzini (1871–1940), a wildly popular soprano whose tempestuous love affairs, legal wrangles, and professional triumphs and disappointments were the stuff of legend. In 1907, there was a dispute over Tetrazzini's contract with the Metropolitan Opera. An injunction was sought to prevent her from singing in any theater until the dispute was resolved. Headed for San Francisco and asked about the injunction, the feisty diva said she would sing in the streets if she had to. Although an injunction was never issued, on Christmas Eve 1910, in front of the San Francisco Chronicle building, Tetrazzini sang before an estimated quarter of a million people. This dish probably dates from that time.

1. Melt the butter in a large saucepan over medium heat. Sauté the mushrooms and shallots in the butter until the mushrooms give up their juice, about 5 minutes. Stir in the flour until you have a paste. Add the broth, milk, and sherry, and stir until smooth and thick.

2. If you are using fresh green beans, steam over boiling water until just barely tender, about 3 minutes. Add the chicken and green beans to the sauce and season generously with salt and pepper.

3. Preheat the oven to 350°F. Lightly grease a 9- by 13-inch baking dish with oil.

4. Bring a large pot of salted water to a boil. Cook the pasta in the water until al dente. Drain well. Mix the pasta into the creamed chicken mixture. Mix in the almonds and parsley. Transfer half the mixture to the prepared baking dish. Sprinkle with half the cheese. Top with the remaining mixture and finish with the remaining cheese.

5. Bake for 30 minutes until the topping is bubbling and hot. Serve hot.

4 tablespoons butter

½ pound mushrooms, sliced

2 shallots, minced

½ cup unbleached all-purpose flour

3 cups chicken broth (see page 62)

½ cup milk

3 tablespoons dry sherry

2 cups fresh or frozen frenched green beans

4 cups shredded or chopped cooked chicken or turkey

Salt and freshly ground black pepper

¾ pound thin spaghetti or vermicelli

½ cup toasted slivered almonds

¼ cup chopped fresh parsley

1 cup freshly grated Parmesan

OVEN-BAKED POT ROAST WITH VEGETABLES

SERVES 4 TO 6

Although pot roast takes several hours to bake, it is mostly unattended time. It can also be made ahead of time; when the meat and vegetables are tender, remove the pot from the oven and refrigerate overnight. Skim off the fat and reheat the meat and vegetables in the pan juices.

1. Mix together the garlic, thyme, rosemary, and salt and pepper; rub the mixture all over the meat. Let stand for 15 to 20 minutes, while you preheat the oven to 275°F.

2. Heat the oil in a large Dutch oven over medium-high heat. Add the meat and brown all over until dark and crusty, about 20 minutes.

3. Remove the meat from the Dutch oven. Pour off all but 2 tablespoons fat. Add the onions and celery, and sauté until the vegetables are softened, 3 minutes. Add the broth and wine, bring to a boil, and cook until the liquid is reduced to about 1½ cups. Return the meat to the pot, add the bay leaves, and cover.

4. Bake for 3 hours, until the meat is almost tender, turning the meat every half hour. The timing varies, depending on the cut and shape of the roast. You can tell the meat is tender if a fork will pierce the meat without too much resistance and the juices run clear. Add the potatoes, carrots, rutabaga, and parsnip, and continue to bake until the meat and vegetables are tender, about 1 hour more.

5. Remove the meat and vegetables to a platter and cover to keep warm. Pour the pan juices into a glass measure. Discard the bay leaves and skim off any fat from the surface. Return to the pan and bring to a boil. Make a paste of 1 tablespoon flour and 1 tablespoon water for every cup of liquid — you will have 3 to 4 cups. Stir in the flour paste and allow to boil until thickened.

6. Slice the meat; serve with the vegetables and gravy.

- 4 garlic cloves, minced
- 2 tablespoons chopped fresh thyme, or 1 tablespoon dried
- 1 tablespoon chopped fresh or dried rosemary leaves

  Salt and freshly ground black pepper
- 1 beef chuck or rump roast (3–5 pounds)
- 3 tablespoons extra-virgin olive or canola oil
- 2 onions, finely chopped
- 2 celery stalks, finely chopped
- 1½ cups beef broth
- ½ cup dry red wine
- 2 bay leaves
- 1 pound red potatoes, cubed
- 2–3 carrots, cubed
- 1 rutabaga, peeled and cubed
- 1 parsnip, peeled and cubed
- 3–4 tablespoons unbleached all-purpose flour
- 3–4 tablespoons water

CORNED BEEF AND CABBAGE

SERVES 4 TO 6

It's a pity that corned beef and cabbage is reserved for St. Patrick's Day, because this is a one-dish wonder that most people love — provided it is cooked properly. The secret is to never allow the water to boil too vigorously. It must be simmered — very, very gently. To accomplish this, I like to cook the corned beef in a slow oven.

1 Preheat the oven to 250°F.

2 Place the corned beef in a large ovenproof pot and cover with water. Add the pickling spice. Cover tightly and bake for about 3 hours, until the meat is tender when poked with a fork.

3 Let the meat cool in the cooking liquid for 15 minutes.

4 Place the meat on a platter and cover with a tent of foil.

5 Place the pot on top of the stove and bring the cooking liquid to a boil. Add the potatoes and carrots, and simmer for about 20 minutes. The vegetables should be firm but tender. Add the cabbage and simmer for 5 to 10 minutes more, until all the vegetables are tender.

6 Remove the vegetables with a slotted spoon to a serving bowl. Cover and keep warm. Return the meat to the cooking liquid to reheat, about 5 minutes.

7 Slice the meat against the grain and serve with the vegetables, passing mustard at the table.

6 pounds corned beef brisket

2 tablespoons mixed pickling spices

4–6 potatoes, peeled and quartered

2–3 carrots, peeled and quartered

1 head cabbage, cut into wedges

Mustard, to serve

IRISH STEW

SERVES 4 TO 6

"Then hurrah for an Irish Stew, that will stick to your belly like glue." This bit of culinary wisdom was found on an English broadsheet around 1800. The first written reference to Irish stew is in Lord Byron's poem "Devil's Drive" (1814), in which he wrote, "The Devil . . . dined on . . . a rebel or so in an Irish stew." Mutton or goat plus potatoes and onions are the most common ingredients found in an Irish stew. Traditionally, the meat, potatoes, and onions were layered in a Dutch oven, broth or water was poured in, then the pot was covered tightly and hung over a fire to simmer slowly for hours. This version uses lamb and a slightly more refined cooking method.

1 Pour boiling water over the onions in a bowl and set aside; this will make the onions easy to peel.

2 In a large bowl, combine the flour and thyme. Season generously with salt and pepper and mix well. Add the meat and toss to coat.

3 Heat the oil in a large skillet over medium-high heat. Shake the excess flour off the meat and add enough pieces to fit in a single layer. Brown on both sides, about 4 minutes per side, and transfer to a roasting pan. Continue until all the meat is browned.

4 Preheat the oven to 300°F.

5 Pour the broth into the skillet and stir to scrape up any browned bits. Pour over the meat in the roasting pan. Peel the onions and add to the roasting pan. Scatter the potatoes, rutabagas, and carrots in the pan. Cover tightly with aluminum foil.

6 Bake for 2 hours, stirring every half hour or so, until the meat and vegetables are completely tender. Taste and adjust the seasonings. Serve hot.

1 pound pearl onions

1 cup unbleached all-purpose flour

1 tablespoon dried thyme

Salt and freshly ground black pepper

3 tablespoons canola or other vegetable oil

4 pounds lamb stew meat with bones (from the neck and shoulder)

3 cups beef or chicken broth (see page 62)

1 pound new potatoes, quartered or cut into eighths, depending on size

1 rutabaga or 2–3 turnips, peeled and diced

2–3 carrots, sliced ½ inch thick

BRAISED LAMB SHANKS WITH VEGETABLES

SERVES 4

These lamb shanks are cooked in the style of osso buco, and the flavor is rich and hearty. If you are so inclined, polenta makes a terrific accompaniment, but a loaf of bread is all that is really needed.

1 Cover the onions with boiling water and set aside to cool. This will make the onions easy to peel.

2 Preheat the oven to 275°F. Set out a large roasting pan.

3 Preheat a dry skillet over high heat. Place the lamb shanks in the skillet, sprinkle with salt and pepper and brown on all sides, about 5 minutes per side. Transfer the lamb to the roasting pan.

4 Pour the broth and wine into the skillet and bring to a boil, stirring to scrape up any browned bits. Pour the liquid into the roasting pan. Add the tomatoes, rosemary, thyme, garlic, and bay leaves.

5 Peel the onions. Add to the roasting pan, along with the potatoes and carrots. Mix gently. Season to taste with salt and pepper. Tightly cover the pan with aluminum foil.

6 Bake for about 2 hours, until the meat is almost falling off the bone. Remove the bay leaves and serve.

1 pound white pearl or boiling onions

4 lamb shanks, ¾–1 pound each
Salt and freshly ground black pepper

1 cup beef or chicken broth (see page 62)

½ cup white or red wine

1 can (28 ounces) diced tomatoes with juice

1 tablespoon chopped fresh rosemary

1 tablespoon chopped fresh thyme

4 garlic cloves, minced

2 bay leaves

2 pounds new potatoes, quartered or cut into eighths

2 carrots, sliced ½ inch thick

ONE-DISH TIP:
LOW AND SLOW

When braising tough cuts of meat, such as lamb shanks or pot roast, it is important to keep the temperature low and steady. Don't try to rush the cooking by increasing the temperature — you will only toughen the meat.

PASTITSIO

SERVES 6 TO 8

Pastitsio, sometimes called Greek macaroni and cheese, is perfect for family gatherings and holiday meals. It is easily made ahead and can be reheated before serving. Like lasagna, pastitsio is a layered casserole that holds its shape and can be served in squares.

1. Begin heating a large pot of salted water for the pasta.

2. Heat the oil in a large skillet over medium-high heat. Sauté the onions in the oil until limp, about 3 minutes. Add the lamb and sauté until browned, 8 to 10 minutes, crumbling the meat as it cooks.

3. Stir in the tomato sauce, tomato paste, water, cinnamon, and oregano. Season to taste with salt, pepper, and a little sugar. Bring to a boil, then reduce the heat and simmer.

4. Cook the pasta in the boiling water until just al dente. Drain.

5. To make the white sauce, melt the butter over medium heat in a small saucepan. Stir in the flour to make a smooth paste. Cook for about 1 minute. Stir in the milk, a little at a time, until all the milk has been added and the sauce is smooth. Cook, stirring constantly, until the sauce is thick and smooth.

6. Beat the eggs in a small bowl. Add ½ cup of the hot white sauce, 1 tablespoon at a time, to warm the eggs. Stir the warmed egg mixture into the white sauce and remove from the heat. Season to taste with salt, pepper, and a grating of fresh nutmeg.

7. Preheat the oven to 350°F. Lightly oil a 9- by 13-inch baking pan.

8. To assemble the casserole, layer half the pasta in the baking pan. Top with half the sauce, then half the Parmesan. Layer the remaining pasta, sauce, and cheese on top. Pour the white sauce over all.

9. Bake, uncovered, for about 40 minutes, or until hot and lightly browned.

10. Let stand for 10 minutes before serving.

- 2 tablespoons extra-virgin olive oil
- 2 onions, finely chopped
- 2 pounds ground lamb or beef
- 1 can (8 ounces) unseasoned tomato sauce
- 1 can (6 ounces) tomato paste
- 1 cup water
- ½ teaspoon ground cinnamon
- ½ teaspoon dried oregano
-   Salt and freshly ground black pepper
-   Pinch sugar, or to taste
- 1 pound tube-shaped pasta, such as penne
- 3 tablespoons butter
- ¼ cup unbleached all-purpose flour
- 3½ cups milk
- 3 eggs, beaten
-   Freshly grated nutmeg
- 1½ cups freshly grated Parmesan

MOUSSAKA

SERVES 6 TO 8

A layered casserole of eggplant and lamb in a tomato sauce, moussaka is Greek in origin but popular throughout the Middle East. It is another great make-ahead dish, perfect for festive gatherings.

1 Heat 1 tablespoon of the oil in a large skillet over medium-high heat. Sauté the lamb, onion, and garlic in the oil until the lamb loses its pink color, about 10 minutes. Drain off as much fat as possible.

2 Stir in the tomato purée, wine, oregano, and cinnamon. Season to taste with salt, pepper, and sugar. Reduce the heat and let simmer while you prepare the eggplant.

3 Preheat the broiler.

4 Arrange the eggplant in a single layer on the broiler pan. Brush the tops with oil, sprinkle with salt and pepper, and broil until browned, about 7 minutes. Turn, brush the second side with oil, and broil for about 5 minutes, until browned. Repeat with the remaining eggplant. You will have to do this in about three batches. When the broiling is completed, lower the oven temperature to 350°F.

5 To prepare the topping, melt the butter over medium heat in a small saucepan. Stir in the flour to form a smooth paste and cook for 1 minute. Add the milk and cook, stirring frequently until the sauce is smooth and thick. Season to taste with salt, pepper, and a grating of nutmeg.

6 To assemble, layer one-third of the eggplant in a 9-by 13-inch baking dish. Top with a third of the meat sauce and sprinkle with a third of the Parmesan. Repeat to make two more layers with the remaining eggplant, meat sauce, and Parmesan. Spoon the white sauce over the top.

7 Bake for 20 to 30 minutes, until the topping is browned. Serve hot.

Olive oil

1½ pounds ground lamb

1 onion, diced

2 cloves garlic, minced

1 can (28 ounces) tomato purée

½ cup red wine

1 tablespoon dried oregano

1 teaspoon ground cinnamon

Salt and freshly ground black pepper

Pinch sugar

4 eggplants (4–5 pounds), peeled and sliced ³/₈ inch thick

4 tablespoons butter

¼ cup unbleached all-purpose flour

2 cups milk

Freshly grated nutmeg

1 cup freshly grated Parmesan

ROAST PORK WITH SAUERKRAUT

SERVES 4 TO 6

Schweineschlegel mit Kartoffel, Karotte, Zwiebel, und Sauerkraut was thought to bring good luck when eaten on New Year's Day. But the family who owned a pig was guaranteed to eat well throughout the upcoming winter, so maybe the luck was already there. In any case, this is an incredibly simple, incredibly delicious dish — as long as the sauerkraut is of high quality. Choose bottled or bagged sauerkraut from the refrigerated section of the grocery store and skip the canned stuff. Also, don't overcook the pork. Today's lean pork is best roasted until it is medium, not well done. Applesauce is a traditional accompaniment.

1 Preheat the oven to 325°F.

2 Heat the oil in a large skillet over medium-high heat. Add the pork and brown on all sides, about 15 minutes. Remove the pork and place in a large roasting pan. Add the broth to the skillet and deglaze, scraping up any browned bits. Remove from the heat.

3 Mix together the sauerkraut, potatoes, carrots, onions, and caraway seeds. Arrange the sauerkraut mixture around the roast. Pour in the broth. Season generously with pepper. Tightly cover the pan with aluminum foil.

4 Roast for 60 to 90 minutes, until the roast registers 145–150°F on an instant-read thermometer.

5 Remove the meat to a warm platter and let rest for 15 minutes. Keep the vegetables warm, or return to the oven if the potatoes are not tender.

6 Carve the meat and serve with the vegetables.

1 tablespoon canola oil
1 bone-in pork loin roast (3–4 pounds)
½ cup chicken broth (see page 62)
4 pounds sauerkraut, drained
6 medium red potatoes, quartered or cut into eighths
4 carrots, sliced ½ inch thick
2 onions, halved lengthwise and slivered
2 tablespoons caraway seeds
Freshly ground black pepper

HAM & POTATO GRATIN

SERVES 3 OR 4

Dorothy Parker famously commented that "eternity is two people and a ham." Many a home cook must have thought the same as she made one more dish using up the leftover holiday ham. Here's another old-fashioned favorite.

1 Combine the potatoes, leeks, garlic, and thyme in a medium, heavy-bottomed saucepan. Add enough milk to cover the potatoes. Season generously with salt and pepper. Simmer over medium heat, stirring occasionally until the potatoes are tender, about 20 minutes. Taste and add more salt and pepper, if desired (unless the ham is exceptionally salty, it will need plenty).

2 Preheat the oven to 350°F.

3 Grease a 2-quart gratin dish with butter. Using a slotted spoon, make a single layer of potatoes and leeks, then a layer using half the ham. Sprinkle a third of the cheese on top. Repeat the layers, ending with a final layer of cheese. Pour in the milk that the potatoes cooked in.

4 Bake for about 30 minutes, until a golden crust has formed on top and the potatoes are bubbling.

5 Let sit for about 10 minutes, then serve hot.

2½ pounds russet or Yukon gold potatoes (about 6 medium-sized), peeled and thinly sliced

4 leeks or 2 onions, trimmed and thinly sliced

2 garlic cloves, thinly sliced

1 thyme sprig

2–3 cups milk

Salt and freshly ground black pepper

1–2 cups diced ham

1 cup grated Gruyère

POTATO FLOWERS IN HER HAIR

The first cook to think of making a potato gratin is lost to history, but it could have happened at a banquet given by Louis XVI in 1785, at which only potato dishes were served — to encourage the adoption of the potato by French society. Benjamin Franklin was one of the guests and was undoubtedly charmed to see Marie Antoinette wearing potato flowers in her hair.

Flowers, of course, were not sufficient to encourage the population at large to adopt the potato into their diet. Instead, the royal gardens were planted with potatoes under the watchful eyes of armed guards, who were instructed to look the other way when potatoes were stolen by curious peasants. These potatoes were planted in the thieves' gardens and the popularity of the potatoes increased steadily.

SALAD SUPPERS

SOUTHWESTERN RICE & BEAN SALAD

SERVES 4

The earthy flavors of black beans and green olives are well matched by the lime juice and cilantro in this colorful salad. In the summer, garnish it with fresh tomato wedges to add even more color.

1 Combine the rice, corn, beans, peppers, scallions, cilantro, and olives in a large salad bowl. Toss to mix.

2 Add the oil and lime juice and toss to mix. Season generously with salt and pepper. Serve at once. (You can hold the salad in the refrigerator for a few hours, but bring to room temperature before serving.)

"According to a Spanish proverb, four persons are wanted to make a salad: a spendthrift for oil, a miser for vinegar, a counselor for salt, and a madman to stir it all up."
— Abraham Hayward, *The Art of Dining* (1854)

3 cups cooked white or brown rice (from 1 cup uncooked)

2 cups fresh or frozen corn kernels

1 can (15 ounces) black beans, rinsed and drained

1 red bell pepper, finely diced

1 green bell pepper, finely diced

½ cup chopped scallions (white and tender green parts)

½ cup chopped fresh cilantro

¼ cup sliced pimiento-stuffed green olives

2 tablespoons extra-virgin olive oil

3 tablespoons fresh lime juice

Salt and freshly ground black pepper

A GUIDE to
SALAD GREENS

ARUGULA. With a distinctively peppery and slightly bitter flavor, arugula stands out in a salad mix. People either love it or hate it. It has small, lobed, dark green leaves on stems that should be discarded if tough. Look for it also under the names "rocket" and "roquette."

CRESS. Both garden cress and watercress have a peppery tang. Cress is a good substitute for arugula.

ESCAROLE. In the chicory family, escarole has broader leaves than frisée but tastes similar. The leaves on the outside of the rosette are darker and more strongly flavored.

FRISÉE. Also known as curly endive or chicory, frisée has a loose head with dark frilly leaves on the outside of the head and paler ones toward the center. The flavor is bracingly bitter.

LETTUCE. There are dozens of different lettuce varieties, but they fall into four general types.

- *Crisphead* lettuces, such as iceberg, form a firm round head. Each head contains about 90 percent water by weight, which accounts for its insipid flavor. Alone these lettuces make a bland salad, but in a mix of greens, they add a juicy texture and sweet flavor.

- *Romaine* or *cos* lettuces have long, narrow leaves that are dark on the outside and lighter and crisper toward the interior of the head. They offer more flavor than iceberg lettuces while still being crisp and sweet.

- *Butterhead* lettuces include Boston lettuce, butter lettuce, Bibb lettuce and Kentucky limestone lettuce. Their leaves are distinctively soft and crumpled, with a mild, sweet flavor and buttery texture. Butterhead lettuces are quite delicate and wilt almost as soon as they are dressed. A salad that includes butterhead tastes richer and more luxurious than usual.

- *Loose-leaf* lettuces offer the most variety in shape and color. In general, these lettuces are mild, sweet, and somewhat crisp, with colors ranging from pale green to deeply red.

MÂCHE. Mâche also goes by the names of corn salad or field lettuce (because it is found growing wild in corn fields) and lamb's lettuce (because the small, tender, velvety leaves are said to resemble a lamb's tongue). The flavor is delicate and rather nutty; salads that feature mâche are good choices for dressings made with walnut or hazelnut oils.

MESCLUN. From a French word meaning "mixture," mesclun is a combination of baby greens and herbs that may include butter lettuce, mâche, arugula, red leaf lettuce, baby mustard leaves, spinach, dandelion, and herbs; Asian cabbages and greens, such as mizuna, pac choi, and tatsoi; and Red Russian kale when the leaves are "baby."

RADICCHIO. Not a green at all, radicchio is a type of chicory that adds color, texture, and flavor to a salad bowl. Radicchio forms heads that are snowy white with deep maroon markings. The texture is like a very tender cabbage and the flavor is more tart than bitter.

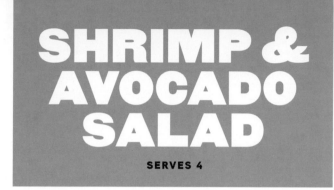

SHRIMP & AVOCADO SALAD

SERVES 4

A Southwestern-style vinaigrette with cilantro and limes brings just the right flavor to this salad of shrimp, avocado, black beans, and peppers. The tortilla chips add extra crunch.

1 Bring a medium saucepan of water to a boil. Add the shrimp, reduce the heat, and cook in barely simmering water for 4 to 5 minutes, until pink and firm. Drain, rinse in cool water, and peel.

2 In a large mixing bowl, combine the shrimp, beans, avocado, carrot, bell peppers, jicama, cucumber, scallions, and chile. Toss lightly to mix.

3 Prepare the salad by making a bed of lettuce on individual plates. Surround the lettuce with the chips.

4 To make the vinaigrette, combine the lime juice, vinegar, garlic, and cilantro in a small bowl. Whisk in the oil. Season to taste with salt and pepper.

5 Pour the vinaigrette over the shrimp salad and toss lightly to mix. Taste and add salt and pepper, if desired.

6 To serve, heap the shrimp salad in the middle of the lettuce beds. Serve at once.

SALAD

1 pound shrimp

1 can (15 ounces) black beans, rinsed and drained

1 avocado, peeled and diced

1 carrot, julienned

1 red bell pepper, julienned

1 green bell pepper, julienned

1 cup julienned jicama

½ English cucumber, julienned

½ cup julienned scallions (white and tender green parts)

1 teaspoon minced fresh red or green chile

1–2 heads butter lettuce

6 ounces tortilla chips

CILANTRO-LIME VINAIGRETTE

3 tablespoons fresh lime juice

1 tablespoon white wine vinegar

2 garlic cloves, minced

½ cup chopped fresh cilantro

2 tablespoons extra-virgin olive oil

Salt and freshly ground black pepper

VIETNAMESE SHRIMP & NOODLE SALAD

SERVES 4

With no oil in the dressing, this salad is light — perfect for hot weather, terrific for a heart-healthy diet. The rice noodles vary in terms of best cooking methods. Follow the instructions on the package if they differ from the ones provided below.

1 Bring a large pot of water to a boil. Remove from the heat and add the rice vermicelli. Leave in the water for 3 to 5 minutes, until al dente. Rinse in cold water and drain well.

2 To make the dressing, combine the fish sauce, vinegar, sugar, and garlic in a small saucepan. Heat gently, stirring constantly, until the sugar is dissolved. Set aside to cool.

3 Bring a medium saucepan of water to a boil. Add the shrimp and lemon, reduce the heat, and poach the shrimp in barely simmering water until pink and firm, 3 to 5 minutes. Drain, discard the lemon, and set aside.

4 Place the rice noodles in a large mixing bowl and pour in half the dressing. Toss well. Add the shrimp, carrot, cucumber, and scallion; toss again.

5 Serve immediately, or hold for up to 1 day by refrigerating in an airtight container. To serve, divide the salad among individual dinner plates and garnish each with a sprinkling of cilantro and peanuts. Pass the remaining dressing at the table.

1 pound rice vermicelli

⅔ cup Asian fish sauce

½ cup white vinegar

⅓ cup sugar

2 garlic cloves, minced

1 pound medium shrimp, peeled

½ lemon

1 carrot, julienned

1 cucumber, peeled, seeded, and julienned

1 scallion (white and tender green parts), chopped

2–3 tablespoons chopped fresh cilantro

2–3 tablespoons chopped roasted peanuts

"To make a good salad is to be a brilliant diplomat: one must know exactly how much oil one must put with one's vinegar."
— Oscar Wilde (1856–1900)

VIETNAMESE SHRIMP & VEGETABLE SALAD

SERVES 4

A snappy mix of shrimp, carrots, cucumbers, daikon (a giant white radish), and herbs makes a perfect warm-weather salad. The dressing, a classic Vietnamese dipping sauce, contains no oil — just fish sauce, white vinegar, sugar, and garlic.

1 First, make the dressing. Combine the fish sauce, vinegar, sugar, and garlic in a small saucepan. Heat gently, stirring constantly, until the sugar is dissolved. Set aside to cool.

2 Bring a medium saucepan of water to a boil. Add the shrimp and lemon, reduce the heat, and poach the shrimp in barely simmering water until pink and firm, 3 to 5 minutes. Drain and discard the lemon.

3 Combine the carrots, cucumber, and daikon radish with the salt in a medium bowl and let stand for 10 minutes. Rinse the salt off with cold running water and drain well. Pat dry with paper towels.

4 Combine the shrimp and salted vegetables in a large bowl. Pour in about two-thirds of the dressing. Toss well. (The salad can be held in the refrigerator for several hours at this point, but bring to room temperature before serving.)

5 To serve, arrange the lettuce, basil, cilantro, and mint on individual dinner plates or a large serving platter. Spoon the shrimp and dressed vegetables on top. Pass the remaining dressing at the table.

DRESSING

9 tablespoons Asian fish sauce

9 tablespoons white vinegar

6 tablespoons sugar

2 teaspoons finely chopped garlic

SALAD

2 pounds medium-sized shrimp, peeled

½ lemon

3 cups julienned carrots

3 cups julienned English (hot house) cucumber

2 cups julienned peeled daikon radish

1 tablespoon salt

6 cups finely shredded romaine lettuce

1 cup fresh basil leaves

1 cup fresh cilantro leaves

1 cup fresh mint leaves

SHRIMP SALAD WITH SOY-CHILI VINAIGRETTE

SERVES 4

A spicy combination of noodles, shrimp, and Chinese vegetables, dressed in a delightfully bold sauce. The heat comes from a jar of chili paste with garlic, which is readily found wherever Asian foods are sold. Chili paste loses potency over time. Be sure to taste the dressing to add the perfect amount.

1 Bring a medium saucepan of water to a boil. Add the shrimp and lemon, reduce the heat, and poach the shrimp in barely simmering water until pink and firm, 3 to 5 minutes. Drain and discard the lemon.

2 Cook the noodles in plenty of boiling salted water until just al dente, 2 to 3 minutes for fresh noodles, 7 to 9 minutes for linguine. Drain. Rinse briefly under cold running water. Drain well. Toss with the sesame oil.

3 Combine the noodles with the shrimp, snow peas, scallions, corn, and carrot. Toss to mix.

4 To make the vinaigrette, combine the soy sauce, broth, vinegar, sugar, 1 teaspoon of the chili paste, garlic, and sesame oil in a small bowl and blend well with a fork. Taste by dipping a noodle into the vinaigrette. Add more chili paste as desired. (The salad and vinaigrette can be refrigerated in separate containers for several hours at this point, but bring to room temperature before serving.)

5 Toss the salad with the vinaigrette and serve.

1 pound shrimp, peeled

½ lemon

1 pound fresh Chinese noodles or ¾ pound dried linguine

1 tablespoon Asian sesame oil

½ pound snow peas, trimmed (2 cups)

6 scallions (white and tender green parts), julienned

1 can (15 ounces) baby corn, drained, rinsed, and cut into bite-size pieces

1 carrot, julienned

SOY-CHILI VINAIGRETTE

¼ cup soy sauce

¼ cup chicken broth (see page 62)

3 tablespoons rice wine vinegar

2 teaspoons sugar

1–3 teaspoons chili paste with garlic

1 garlic clove, minced

1 teaspoon Asian sesame oil

TUSCAN TUNA SALAD WITH WHITE BEANS

SERVES 4

For a dinner you can toss together in less than 20 minutes, nothing beats this summery tuna salad. It needs only a jug of wine and a loaf of bread to complete it. If you can also provide a summer breeze, a lovely view from a shaded porch and the scent of flowers in the air, so much the better. Sweet vine-ripened tomatoes and fresh basil are a must to properly complement the briny tuna and earthy beans.

1 Combine the tuna, scallions, garlic, basil, capers, vinegar, and oil in a large salad bowl. Toss to mix. Gently fold in the beans. Season to taste with salt and pepper. (The salad can be refrigerated for up to 4 hours at this point; bring to room temperature before serving.)

2 Just before serving, add the greens and tomatoes to the tuna mixture, toss, and serve.

1 can (6.5–7.5 ounces) oil-packed tuna (preferably imported from Italy), drained and flaked

4 scallions (white and tender green parts), chopped

3 garlic cloves, minced

½ cup chopped fresh basil

2 tablespoons capers, drained

3 tablespoons red wine vinegar

¼ cup extra-virgin olive oil

1 can (15 ounces) cannellini beans, rinsed and drained

Salt and freshly ground black pepper

12 cups torn mixed salad greens

4 tomatoes, chopped

SHRIMP & WHITE BEAN SALAD

SERVES 4

A healthy combination of shrimp and white beans is dressed with a roasted garlic vinaigrette in this good-for-you salad. Roasting mellows the garlic and brings out a sweet, nutty flavor. The dressing is also good on Caesar salads.

1 To make the vinaigrette, preheat the oven to 450°F.

2 Remove the papery outer skin from the garlic bulb. Slice off the top of the bulb to expose the tips of the cloves. Place the bulb in a small ovenproof bowl and pour the broth over the bulb. Roast for about 30 minutes, basting once or twice, until the cloves are soft and browned. Remove the garlic from the bowl and let cool. (If you are in a hurry, separate the cloves to speed the cooling process.)

3 When the garlic is cool enough to handle, squeeze out the cloves from the skins. In a blender, combine the garlic purée with the oil, wine, vinegar, and salt to taste. Process until smooth. (Stored in an airtight container, the vinaigrette will keep for up to 4 days in the refrigerator.)

4 Bring a medium saucepan of water to a boil. Add the shrimp, reduce the heat, and cook in barely simmering water for 4 to 5 minutes, until pink and firm. Drain, rinse in cool water, and peel.

5 Combine the beans and half the salad dressing in a medium bowl.

6 To serve, place a bed of arugula on individual plates. Arrange the tomatoes around the outside. Spoon the beans onto the center of the greens. Arrange the shrimp on top of the beans, then top with the onion and capers. Drizzle with the remaining dressing and serve.

ROASTED GARLIC VINAIGRETTE

- 1 whole head garlic
- ¼ cup chicken broth (see page 62)
- 3 tablespoons extra-virgin olive oil
- 3 tablespoons white wine
- 1 tablespoon red wine vinegar
  Salt

SALAD

- 1½ pounds medium-sized shrimp
- 1 can (19 ounces) cannellini beans, drained and rinsed
- 12 cups torn arugula
- 4 medium-sized tomatoes, cut into wedges
- ½ cup thinly sliced Vidalia or other sweet onion
- 2 teaspoons capers, drained

ONE-DISH TIP:
GREEN MATH

1 pound greens =
6 cups loosely packed

MEDITERRANEAN TUNA VEGETABLE SALAD

SERVES 4

Another take on tuna salad is to combine it with plenty of crunchy vegetables and mixed greens. Hold the mayo, please!

1 Blanch the green beans in a small saucepan of boiling water for 45 seconds. Drain, plunge into cold water to stop the cooking, and drain again.

2 Combine the green beans, chickpeas, artichoke hearts, carrot, green pepper, olives, onion, and capers in a large salad bowl. Toss gently to mix.

3 Whisk together the vinegar, basil, and garlic in a small bowl. Whisk in the oil until fully incorporated. Pour over the vegetables. If you have the time, set the salad aside for at least 30 minutes at room temperature, or for up to 8 hours in the refrigerator, tossing occasionally, to allow the flavors to develop.

4 Just before serving, add the tuna and tomatoes to the salad and toss well. Season to taste with salt and pepper. Add the greens and toss again. Taste and adjust the seasonings, and serve.

1 cup green beans, cut into 1½-inch pieces

1 can (15 ounces) chickpeas, rinsed and drained

1 can (14 ounces) artichoke hearts, rinsed, drained, and quartered

1 carrot, julienned

½ green bell pepper, thinly sliced

½ cup brined-cured black olives, such as kalamata

¼ cup diced red onion

1–2 tablespoons capers, drained

¼ cup red wine vinegar

¼ cup chopped fresh basil

4 garlic cloves, minced

5 tablespoons extra-virgin olive oil

1 can (6.5–7.5 ounces) oil-packed tuna, preferably imported from Italy, drained and flaked

4 plum tomatoes, diced

Salt and freshly ground black pepper

12 cups torn mixed salad greens

TROUT, ASPARAGUS & NEW POTATO SALAD

SERVES 4

Although it has become a year-round item in the supermarket, nothing beats the fresh taste of local asparagus each spring. Pair the spears with new potatoes and pan-seared trout for a fresh spring treat.

1 Cover the potatoes with salted water in a medium saucepan. Bring to a boil. Boil gently until the potatoes are just tender, about 8 minutes. Remove from the heat and set aside.

2 Steam the asparagus until just tender, 3 to 4 minutes. Remove from the heat, plunge into cold water to stop the cooking, and drain well.

3 Heat 1 tablespoon of the oil in a large skillet over medium-high heat. Sauté the shallot in the oil until limp, about 2 minutes. Add the asparagus, potatoes, and thyme, and toss to coat with the oil. Add the broth and vinegar. Bring to a boil. Transfer to a large bowl and season to taste with salt and pepper.

4 Heat 1 tablespoon of the oil in the skillet. Add two of the fillets in a single layer and cook, turning once, until golden brown on both sides, about 4 minutes total. Transfer to a plate. Repeat, using the remaining oil and fillets.

5 Arrange the salad greens on individual plates. Place one fillet on each plate. Spoon the asparagus salad around the edges. Combine any pan juices with any dressing remaining in the bowl that held the asparagus salad, drizzle over the individual salads, and serve at once.

1½ pounds new potatoes, quartered or cut into eighths

1 pound asparagus, trimmed and cut into 2-inch lengths

3 tablespoons extra-virgin olive oil

1 shallot, minced

2 teaspoons chopped fresh thyme, or 1 teaspoon dried

½ cup chicken broth (see page 62)

1 tablespoon balsamic vinegar
  Salt and freshly ground black pepper

4 trout fillets (4–5 ounces each)

12 cups torn mixed salad greens

POACHED SALMON SALAD WITH CUCUMBER SAUCE

SERVES 4

Here is a quintessential spring dish with fresh salmon on a bed of peppery watercress and asparagus, topped with a light sauce of cucumber and yogurt.

1 Place the salmon in a large saucepan and cover with cold water. Add the salt and bring just to a boil. Turn off the heat and let stand until the fish is completely cooked through, about 8 minutes. Remove the fish from the water and let cool to room temperature. (If desired, the fish can be refrigerated for several hours at this point. Bring to room temperature before proceeding.)

2 Steam the asparagus over boiling water until barely tender, 3 to 4 minutes. Plunge immediately into cold water to stop the cooking, and drain well.

3 To make the sauce, stir together the yogurt, cucumber, scallions, parsley, and dill. Season to taste with salt and pepper; adjust the other ingredients to taste.

4 Arrange the watercress on individual plates. Arrange the salmon and asparagus on top. Pour a saddle of cucumber sauce over each fillet and pass the remaining sauce at the table.

4 salmon fillets (6 ounces each), skin removed

1 tablespoon salt

1 pound asparagus, trimmed

HERBED CUCUMBER SAUCE

1½ cups plain yogurt

1 English (hothouse) cucumber, finely chopped

2 scallions (white and tender green parts), chopped

¼ cup chopped fresh parsley

1 tablespoon chopped fresh dill or tarragon

Salt and freshly ground black pepper

2 bunches watercress, tough stems removed

GRILLED CHICKEN CAESAR SALAD

SERVES 4

The Caesar salad was invented in a restaurant — in Tijuana, Mexico, by Caesar Cardini in 1924, to be precise — and has long been a staple of restaurants. Because the dressing traditionally includes a raw egg, it makes most home cooks nervous. In this version, the raw egg and much of the oil is replaced by tofu. It works surprising well to create a creamy dressing.

1. To make the croutons, heat the oil in a large skillet over medium heat. Add the bread cubes and garlic. Season to taste with salt and pepper. Fry, stirring occasionally, until the cubes are crisp and golden, 20 to 30 minutes. Let cool in the pan. (The croutons can be made in advance and stored in an airtight jar at room temperature for up to 4 days.)

2. To make the dressing, combine the tofu, water, anchovies, garlic, vinegar, and mustard in a blender and process until smooth.

3. Prepare a medium-hot fire in a charcoal or gas grill, with the rack set 3 to 4 inches above the coals.

4. Combine the oil, garlic, and rosemary in a small bowl. Brush over the chicken. When the coals are medium-hot, grill the chicken for about 7 minutes per side, or until firm and white throughout.

5. Combine the lettuce and croutons in a large salad bowl. Cut the chicken into 1-inch strips and add to the bowl. Pour on the dressing; toss well. Sprinkle with the Parmesan, grind on some pepper, toss, and serve.

GARLIC CROUTONS

- 3 tablespoons extra-virgin olive oil
- ½ pound slightly stale Italian, French, or other white bread, cut into ½-cubes
- 4 garlic cloves, minced
  Salt and freshly ground black pepper

CREAMY CAESAR DRESSING

- 6 ounces silken tofu
- ¼ cup water
- 1 can (2 ounces) anchovy fillets packed in oil (do not drain)
- 2 garlic cloves
- 3 tablespoons red wine vinegar
- 1 teaspoon Dijon mustard

SALAD

- 1 tablespoon extra-virgin olive oil
- 2 garlic cloves, minced
- 1 teaspoon fresh or dried rosemary
- 1 pound boneless, skinless chicken breasts
- 16 cups torn romaine lettuce leaves
- ¼ cup freshly grated Parmesan
  Freshly ground black pepper

CHICKEN NOODLE SALAD WITH PEANUT DRESSING

SERVES 4

Peanut noodles are often found on the appetizer menu of Chinese restaurants. But add cooked chicken and vegetables and you have a pasta salad — Chinese style.

1 Place the chicken in a medium saucepan and cover with water. Add the garlic, ginger, and 4 tablespoons of the rice vinegar. Bring just to a boil, lower the heat, and poach the chicken in barely simmering water until firm and white throughout, about 15 minutes. Cool in the cooking liquid.

2 Meanwhile, cook the noodles according to the package directions until tender but firm to the bite, 2 to 3 minutes for fresh, about 5 minutes for dried. Drain and rinse with cold water. Toss with 1 tablespoon of the sesame oil.

3 In a blender, combine the peanut butter with ½ cup of the chicken-cooking liquid. Add the remaining 2 tablespoons rice wine vinegar, the remaining 1 tablespoon sesame oil, the soy sauce, vinegar, Worcestershire sauce, 1 teaspoon of the chili paste, and sugar. Blend well. Dip a noodle in the sauce to taste for seasoning, and add more chili paste, soy sauce, or vinegar as desired.

4 Remove the chicken from the cooking liquid and julienne. (The chicken, noodles, and dressing can be refrigerated in separate containers for several hours at this point. Bring to room temperature before proceeding.)

5 Combine the chicken, noodles, and dressing in a large salad bowl. Toss well. Taste and adjust the seasoning as needed. Arrange the cucumber, carrot, and scallions on top and serve.

¾ pound boneless, skinless chicken breast

2 garlic cloves

1 piece fresh ginger (1 inch long), sliced

6 tablespoons Chinese rice wine vinegar

1 pound fresh Chinese egg noodles or ¾ pound dried vermicelli

2 tablespoons Asian sesame oil

¼ cup smooth peanut butter

3 tablespoons soy sauce, or more to taste

1 tablespoon rice vinegar

1 tablespoon Worcestershire sauce

1–2 teaspoons Chinese chili paste with garlic, or more to taste

2 tablespoons sugar, or more to taste

1 English (hot house) cucumber, julienned

1 carrot, julienned

1 cup julienned scallions (white and tender green parts)

CURRIED RICE & CHICKEN SALAD

SERVES 4

Bold and exotic is the only way to describe this combination of rice, chicken, apples, peas, and mint, dressed with a tangy mango vinaigrette.

1 Wash the rice in several changes of water until the water runs clear. Drain well.

2 Heat the oil over medium heat. Add the rice, onion, garlic, and curry powder. Sauté until the rice appears opaque, about 4 minutes. Add the salt and water, cover, and bring to a boil. Reduce the heat to low and simmer until the rice is tender and all the water is absorbed, about 15 minutes. Fluff with a fork and transfer to a large salad bowl to cool.

3 When the rice is cool, add the chicken, green pepper, peas, apple, scallions, and mint. Mix well.

4 To make the vinaigrette, combine the chutney, vinegar, oil, mustard, and honey in a blender. Process until well combined. Season to taste with salt and pepper.

5 Pour the vinaigrette over the salad and toss well. Taste, adjust the seasonings, and serve.

SALAD

- 2 cups uncooked white rice (preferably long-grain)
- 2 tablespoons canola oil
- ¼ cup minced onion
- 2 garlic cloves, minced
- 1 tablespoon curry powder
- 1 teaspoon salt
- 3¾ cups water
- 2 cups diced cooked chicken or turkey
- ½ green bell pepper, diced
- 1 cup fresh or frozen green peas
- 1 apple, cored and diced (do not peel)
- ¼ cup chopped scallions (white and tender green parts)
- ¼ cup chopped fresh mint

CHUTNEY VINAIGRETTE

- ¾ cup mango chutney
- 2 tablespoons cider vinegar
- 1 tablespoon canola oil
- 1 teaspoon Dijon mustard
- 1 teaspoon honey
- Salt and freshly ground black pepper

CHICKEN PASTA SALAD

SERVES 4

Turn a classic chicken salad into a pasta salad for kids of all ages.

1 Cook the pasta in a large pot of boiling salted water until just done. Drain and rinse thoroughly to cook. Toss the pasta with the oil.

2 While the pasta is cooking, poach the chicken. Bring water (enough to cover the chicken) to a boil with the garlic and wine. Poach the chicken in barely simmering liquid for about 15 minutes, until done through. Remove from the poaching liquid and let cool.

3 Add the celery, carrot, pepper, and scallion to the pasta. Dice the chicken and add to the pasta.

4 To make the dressing, combine the mayonnaise, lemon juice, parsley, and dill in a food processor and process until smooth.

5 Pour the dressing over the salad and mix well. Mix in the grapes and walnuts. Season to taste with salt and pepper. Serve immediately.

¾ pound rotini or other small pasta

1 tablespoon extra-virgin olive oil

1 boneless, skinless chicken breast

2 garlic cloves

2 tablespoons dry white wine

1 celery stalk, diced

1 carrot, grated

½ green bell pepper, diced

1 scallion (white and tender green parts), chopped

½ cup mayonnaise

5 tablespoons fresh lemon juice

1 cup chopped fresh parsley

2 tablespoons chopped fresh dill

1 cup green or red seedless grapes, halved if large

⅓ cup chopped walnuts

Salt and freshly ground black pepper

TURKEY & WILD RICE SALAD

SERVES 4

Having leftovers after Thanksgiving doesn't mean you have to be stuck with sandwiches for days on end. Here's a fresh take on holiday flavors as a light, healthy salad.

1 To make the vinaigrette, combine the cranberry sauce, shallots, vinegar, and orange juice in a blender and process until smooth. With the motor running, slowly drizzle in the oil and process until it is completely incorporated.

2 To make the salad, combine the turkey, rice, celery, and onion in a large salad bowl. Pour in the vinaigrette and toss well. Add the greens, gently toss again, and serve.

CRANBERRY VINAIGRETTE

1   cup jellied cranberry sauce

2   shallots, chopped

2   tablespoons raspberry or other fruited vinegar or balsamic vinegar

2   tablespoons fresh orange juice

¼   cup walnut or extra-virgin olive oil

SALAD

3   cups cooked diced turkey

2   cups cooked wild rice (from ⅔ cup uncooked)

2   celery stalks, thinly sliced

½   cup thinly sliced red onion

10–12   cups torn mixed salad greens

ANTIPASTO PASTA SALAD

SERVES 4 TO 6

So named because it contains all the ingredients of a traditional American-style antipasto plate — pickled vegetables, capicola, cheese, onions, and tomatoes. Capicola (cured pork shoulder) is available at the delicatessen counter of most supermarkets.

1 Cook the pasta in a large pot of boiling salted water until just done. Drain and rinse thoroughly to cool. Place in a large mixing bowl and toss with 1 tablespoon of the olive oil.

2 Combine the mozzarella, capicola, tomatoes, onion, pickled vegetables, and oregano in a separate large mixing bowl and toss well.

3 Whisk together the vinegar and remaining 4 tablespoons olive oil in a small bowl. Pour over the capicola mixture and toss. (The salad can be held for a few hours by refrigerating the pasta and vegetable mixture in separate airtight containers. Bring to room temperature before proceeding.)

4 Just before serving, toss the capicola mixture with the pasta. Serve at once.

1 pound ziti, penne, or other tubular pasta

5 tablespoons extra-virgin olive oil

½ pound fresh mozzarella, sliced

¼ pound capicola, cut into cubes

2 large tomatoes, seeded and diced

1 small onion, sliced into rings

1 jar (12-ounce) giardiniera (mixed pickled vegetables), drained and rinsed

1 tablespoon chopped fresh oregano, or 1 teaspoon dried

2 tablespoons red wine vinegar

THAI BEEF NOODLE SALAD

SERVES 4

Surprisingly, this salad holds up well in the refrigerator — perfect for making ahead when everyone in the family is on a different schedule.

1 Rub the steak with the soy sauce and garlic; set aside to marinate. Prepare a medium-hot fire in a charcoal or gas grill, with the rack set 3 to 4 inches above the coals, or preheat the broiler.

2 Bring a large pot of water to a boil. Remove from the heat and add the noodles. Leave in the water for 3 to 5 minutes, until al dente. Rinse in cold water and drain well.

3 To make the dressing, combine the fish sauce, lime juice, and sugar in a small saucepan over low heat. Stir until the sugar dissolves; then remove from the heat.

4 Combine the carrot, green pepper, cucumber, and chile with the noodles. Toss well. Pour in the dressing and toss again.

5 Grill or broil the meat until it reaches the desired doneness. A ½-inch-thick steak will take about 3 minutes per side for medium rare. Let rest for 5 minutes. Slice into thin strips.

6 To serve, place the noodle salad on individual serving plates. Arrange the meat on top, and serve immediately.

¾ pound flank steak, sirloin, or other tender beef cut

1 tablespoon soy sauce

1 garlic clove, minced

1 pound rice vermicelli

½ cup Asian fish sauce

6 tablespoons fresh lime juice

¼ cup sugar

1 carrot, shaved into curls

1 green bell pepper, julienned

1 cucumber, peeled (if desired), seeded, and thinly sliced

1 green chile, seeded (optional) and sliced

ONE-DISH TIP:
USING LEMONGRASS

Lemongrass, which gives Asian dishes a characteristic sour-lemon flavor and fragrance, is gray-green in color and somewhat woody in texture, and it resembles a scallion. Stock up on it and keep the extra in an airtight bag in the freezer. Use only the softer, interior portion of the bottom 4 inches. In a pinch, ¼ teaspoon of finely grated lemon zest can be substituted for a stem of lemongrass, but the flavor is not the same.

THAI BEEF SALAD

SERVES 4

Like many of the best Thai dishes, this salad balances sweet, hot, salty, and sour flavors. Strips of rare grilled steak top crunchy vegetables and cellophane noodles that are dressed with a felicitous combination of fish sauce, lime juice, sugar, hot peppers, and lemongrass.

1. Rub the steak with soy sauce and garlic; set aside to marinate.

2. Prepare a medium-hot fire in a charcoal or gas grill, with the rack set 3 to 4 inches above the coals, or preheat the broiler.

3. To make the dressing, combine the fish sauce, lime juice, sugar, chile, and lemongrass in a small saucepan. Heat gently, stirring, until the sugar dissolves, 1 to 2 minutes. Set aside to cool.

4. Soak the cellophane noodles in hot water to soften, about 5 minutes. Drain and set aside.

5. On individual plates, make a bed of lettuce. On top of the lettuce, arrange the cellophane noodles, then the carrot curls, cucumber, mint, and cilantro, reserving a few tablespoons of the herbs for a garnish.

6. When the coals are medium-hot, grill the steak, turning once, until it reaches the desired doneness. A ½-inch-thick steak will take about 3 minutes per side for medium rare. Let rest for a few minutes, then slice into thin strips.

7. Pour the dressing over the salad. Lay the strips of warm steak on top. Serve at once.

STEAK

1 pound flank steak, sirloin steak, or other tender beef cut

2 tablespoons soy sauce

2 garlic cloves, minced

DRESSING

½ cup Asian fish sauce

½ cup fresh lime juice

6 tablespoons sugar

1 hot chile, minced

1 stem lemongrass, finely chopped

SALAD

3 packages (1.75 ounces each) cellophane noodles

6 cups thinly sliced romaine lettuce

1 carrot, shaved into curls

1 English (hot house) cucumber, julienned

¼ cup chopped fresh mint

¼ cup chopped fresh cilantro

CHINESE PORK & NOODLE SALAD

SERVES 4 TO 6

Chinese barbecue sauce, known as hoisin, is the main flavoring agent for this warm salad. The vegetables are briefly blanched to set the color and to cook out the slightly bitter flavor of the raw bean sprouts.

1 Combine the soy sauce, sherry, and hoisin sauce in a shallow bowl large enough to hold the pork. Add the pork and roll in the marinade to coat. Marinate for 30 minutes at room temperature, or for up to 8 hours in the refrigerator.

2 Prepare a medium-hot fire in a charcoal or gas grill, with the rack set 3 to 4 inches above the coals, or preheat the broiler.

3 Bring a large pot of salted water to a boil. Add the snow peas, bean sprouts, and bok choy, and blanch for 45 seconds. Remove from the water with tongs or a slotted spoon and plunge into ice water to stop the cooking. Return the water to a boil and add the noodles. Cook until just done. Drain and rinse thoroughly to cool. Place in a large bowl and toss with the sesame oil.

4 To make the dressing, in a small bowl, stir together the hoisin sauce, soy sauce, vinegar, and sugar. Add to the pasta and toss.

5 Grill or broil the meat for 3 to 10 minutes per side, depending on thickness. Pork is done when the meat is firm throughout and just barely shows pink. Do not overcook. Let rest for 5 minutes.

6 Cut the meat into matchstick-size pieces. Add to the noodles along with the blanched vegetables and scallions. Toss well to mix. Serve at once.

PORK AND MARINADE

2 tablespoons soy sauce

2 tablespoons dry sherry

1 tablespoon hoisin sauce

1 pound boneless pork tenderloin

SALAD

1 cup snow peas, trimmed (¼ pound)

1 cup bean sprouts

3 large stalks bok choy, sliced

1 pound fresh Chinese noodles or ¾ pound vermicelli

1 tablespoon Asian sesame oil

6 scallions (white and tender green parts), slivered lengthwise, and cut into 2-inch pieces

DRESSING

3 tablespoons hoisin sauce

3 tablespoons soy sauce

2 tablespoons rice wine vinegar

1 teaspoon sugar

TACO SALAD

SERVES 4

There's no need to go to the trouble of deep-frying a tortilla to make a bowl for the salad, as they do in restaurants. Serving this Tex-Mex favorite with tortilla chips provides crunch, without the fuss of deep-frying.

1 Heat a large skillet over medium-high heat. Add the beef, onion, chili powder, and cumin, and cook until the meat no longer shows any pink, stirring frequently, about 8 minutes. Add the beans, diced tomatoes, and salt and pepper to taste. Simmer for at least 15 minutes to blend the flavors.

2 Combine the lettuce, cucumber, red onion, and plum tomatoes in a large bowl. Add the lemon juice, oil, and salt and pepper to taste. Toss well.

3 To serve, place a bed of tortilla chips on each plate. Divide the salad among the plates. Top with the cheese, then the warm chili mixture. Top each with a dollop of sour cream and a sprinkling of chiles. Serve immediately.

¾ pound ground beef

1 small onion, finely chopped

2 tablespoons chili powder

1½ teaspoons ground cumin

1 can (15 ounces) kidney beans, rinsed and drained

1 can (15 ounces) diced tomatoes with juice

Salt and freshly ground black pepper

12 cups chopped lettuce

½ English (hothouse) cucumber, thinly sliced

¼ cup chopped red onion

4 plum tomatoes, chopped

2 tablespoons fresh lemon juice

1 tablespoon extra-virgin olive oil

Tortilla chips

½ cup grated Cheddar or Monterey Jack

Sour cream

2 fresh or canned green chiles, chopped

GERMAN-STYLE POTATO SALAD WITH SAUSAGE

SERVES 4

With the addition of low-fat turkey sausage, this classic warm potato salad can become a one-dish meal. Serve it over greens or on its own with a loaf of rye or pumpernickel bread.

1 Bring a medium saucepan of salted water to a boil. Add the potatoes, cover, and boil gently until just tender, about 8 minutes. Drain.

2 Heat the oil in a large skillet over medium-high heat. Add the sausage and cook until brown, breaking it up into small pieces as it cooks, about 8 minutes. Add the bell pepper, onion, and garlic, and sauté until just tender, about 3 minutes.

3 In a small bowl, combine the broth, vinegar, sugar, flour, and celery seeds, and stir until smooth. Add to the skillet and cook, stirring constantly, until thickened and bubbly.

4 Stir in the potatoes, season to taste with the salt and pepper, and cook for 2 to 3 minutes more, stirring gently, until heated through. Serve warm.

2½ pounds small red potatoes, sliced ¼-inch thick

1 tablespoon extra-virgin olive oil or canola oil

1 pound Italian-style hot turkey sausage, casings removed

1 red bell pepper, diced

½ cup diced red or yellow onion

2 garlic cloves, minced

½ cup chicken broth (see page 62) or water

½ cup white vinegar

1 tablespoon sugar

1 tablespoon unbleached all-purpose flour

½ teaspoon celery seeds

Salt and freshly ground black pepper

INDEX

Numbers in *italic* indicate photographs.

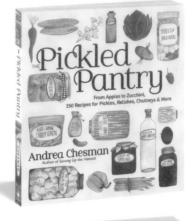
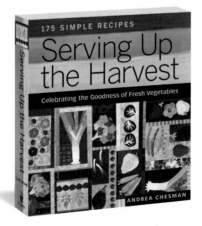